# 50 Homemade Cake and Cupcake Recipes for Home

By: Kelly Johnson

## Table of Contents

- Classic Vanilla Cake
- Chocolate Fudge Cake
- Red Velvet Cake
- Lemon Drizzle Cake
- Carrot Cake with Cream Cheese Frosting
- Banana Bread Cake
- Marble Cake
- Coconut Cake
- Strawberry Shortcake
- Black Forest Cake
- Pineapple Upside-Down Cake
- Funfetti Cake
- Almond Cake
- Tiramisu Cake
- Peanut Butter Chocolate Cake
- Coffee Cake
- Apple Spice Cake
- Pistachio Cake
- Honey Lavender Cake
- Orange Creamsicle Cake
- Raspberry Swirl Cake
- Blueberry Lemon Cake
- Mocha Espresso Cake
- Salted Caramel Cake
- Pumpkin Spice Cake
- Gingerbread Cake
- Almond Joy Cake
- Oreo Cookies and Cream Cake
- Chai Spice Cake
- Key Lime Cake
- Matcha Green Tea Cake
- Mint Chocolate Chip Cake
- White Chocolate Raspberry Cake
- Maple Pecan Cake
- S'mores Cake

- Strawberry Champagne Cake
- Earl Grey Tea Cake
- Cinnamon Roll Cake
- Cranberry Orange Cake
- Neapolitan Cake
- Pineapple Coconut Cake
- Chocolate Peanut Butter Swirl Cake
- Caramel Apple Cake
- Eggnog Cake
- Peppermint Chocolate Cake
- Bourbon Pecan Cake
- Cookies and Cream Cupcakes
- Strawberry Cheesecake Cupcakes
- Lemon Blueberry Cupcakes
- Salted Caramel Cupcakes

**Classic Vanilla Cake**

Ingredients:

- 2 1/2 cups all-purpose flour
- 1 1/2 cups granulated sugar
- 1 cup unsalted butter, softened
- 4 large eggs
- 1 cup whole milk
- 2 teaspoons vanilla extract
- 2 teaspoons baking powder
- 1/2 teaspoon salt

Instructions:

Preheat your oven to 350°F (175°C). Grease and flour two 9-inch round cake pans, or line them with parchment paper.
In a medium bowl, whisk together the flour, baking powder, and salt. Set aside.
In a large mixing bowl, cream together the softened butter and granulated sugar until light and fluffy, using a hand mixer or stand mixer.
Add the eggs one at a time, mixing well after each addition. Stir in the vanilla extract.
Gradually add the dry ingredients to the wet ingredients, alternating with the milk, beginning and ending with the dry ingredients. Mix until just combined; do not overmix.
Divide the batter evenly between the prepared cake pans, smoothing the tops with a spatula.
Bake in the preheated oven for 25-30 minutes, or until a toothpick inserted into the center of the cakes comes out clean.
Remove the cakes from the oven and allow them to cool in the pans for 10 minutes. Then, carefully transfer them to wire racks to cool completely.
Once cooled, frost the cakes with your favorite frosting or decorate as desired.
Enjoy your classic vanilla cake!

**Chocolate Fudge Cake**

Ingredients:

- 1 3/4 cups all-purpose flour
- 1 1/2 cups granulated sugar
- 3/4 cup unsweetened cocoa powder
- 1 1/2 teaspoons baking powder
- 1 1/2 teaspoons baking soda
- 1 teaspoon salt
- 2 large eggs
- 1 cup whole milk
- 1/2 cup vegetable oil
- 2 teaspoons vanilla extract
- 1 cup boiling water

For the Chocolate Fudge Frosting:

- 1 cup unsalted butter, softened
- 4 cups powdered sugar
- 1 cup unsweetened cocoa powder
- 1/2 cup whole milk
- 2 teaspoons vanilla extract

Instructions:

Preheat your oven to 350°F (175°C). Grease and flour two 9-inch round cake pans, or line them with parchment paper.
In a large mixing bowl, sift together the flour, sugar, cocoa powder, baking powder, baking soda, and salt.
Add the eggs, milk, oil, and vanilla extract to the dry ingredients. Beat on medium speed for 2 minutes, scraping down the sides of the bowl as needed.
Stir in the boiling water until the batter is well combined and smooth. The batter will be thin; this is normal.
Pour the batter evenly into the prepared cake pans.
Bake in the preheated oven for 30 to 35 minutes, or until a toothpick inserted into the center of the cakes comes out clean.

Remove the cakes from the oven and allow them to cool in the pans for 10 minutes. Then, carefully transfer them to wire racks to cool completely.

While the cakes are cooling, prepare the chocolate fudge frosting. In a large mixing bowl, beat the softened butter until creamy.

Gradually add the powdered sugar and cocoa powder, alternating with the milk, beating on low speed until well combined and smooth.

Stir in the vanilla extract until the frosting is smooth and creamy.

Once the cakes are completely cool, frost the top of one cake layer with a generous amount of chocolate fudge frosting. Place the second cake layer on top and frost the top and sides of the cake with the remaining frosting.

Slice and serve your delicious chocolate fudge cake. Enjoy!

**Red Velvet Cake**

Ingredients:

For the Cake:

- 2 1/2 cups all-purpose flour
- 1 1/2 cups granulated sugar
- 1 teaspoon baking soda
- 1 teaspoon salt
- 1 teaspoon cocoa powder
- 1 1/2 cups vegetable oil
- 1 cup buttermilk, room temperature
- 2 large eggs, room temperature
- 2 tablespoons red food coloring
- 1 teaspoon vanilla extract
- 1 teaspoon white vinegar

For the Cream Cheese Frosting:

- 16 ounces cream cheese, softened
- 1/2 cup unsalted butter, softened
- 4 cups powdered sugar
- 1 teaspoon vanilla extract

Instructions:

For the Cake:

Preheat your oven to 350°F (175°C). Grease and flour two 9-inch round cake pans.
In a large bowl, sift together the flour, sugar, baking soda, salt, and cocoa powder.
In another bowl, whisk together the vegetable oil, buttermilk, eggs, red food coloring, vanilla extract, and white vinegar until well combined.
Gradually add the wet ingredients to the dry ingredients, mixing until the batter is smooth and well combined.
Divide the batter evenly between the prepared cake pans.
Bake in the preheated oven for 25-30 minutes, or until a toothpick inserted into the center of the cakes comes out clean.
Remove the cakes from the oven and let them cool in the pans for 10 minutes. Then, transfer the cakes to a wire rack to cool completely.

For the Cream Cheese Frosting:

- In a large bowl, beat the cream cheese and butter together until smooth and creamy.
- Gradually add the powdered sugar, one cup at a time, beating well after each addition.
- Stir in the vanilla extract and mix until smooth and creamy.

Assembling the Cake:

- Once the cakes have cooled completely, place one cake layer on a serving plate or cake stand.
- Spread a layer of cream cheese frosting evenly over the top of the first cake layer.
- Place the second cake layer on top and spread the remaining frosting over the top and sides of the cake.
- Optionally, decorate the cake with red velvet cake crumbs or sprinkles.
- Refrigerate the cake for at least 1 hour before serving to allow the frosting to set.
- Slice and serve your delicious red velvet cake, and enjoy!

This red velvet cake is perfect for special occasions, celebrations, or any time you're craving a decadent and indulgent dessert.

**Lemon Drizzle Cake**

Ingredients:

For the Cake:

- 1 3/4 cups all-purpose flour
- 1 1/2 teaspoons baking powder
- 1/2 teaspoon salt
- 1 cup unsalted butter, softened
- 1 cup granulated sugar
- 4 large eggs, room temperature
- Zest of 2 lemons
- 2 tablespoons fresh lemon juice
- 1 teaspoon vanilla extract

For the Drizzle:

- 1/4 cup fresh lemon juice
- 1/4 cup granulated sugar

Instructions:

For the Cake:

Preheat your oven to 350°F (175°C). Grease and flour a 9x5-inch loaf pan.
In a medium bowl, whisk together the flour, baking powder, and salt. Set aside.
In a large bowl, cream together the softened butter and granulated sugar until light and fluffy.
Beat in the eggs, one at a time, until well combined. Add the lemon zest, lemon juice, and vanilla extract, and mix until incorporated.
Gradually add the dry ingredients to the wet ingredients, mixing until just combined. Be careful not to overmix.
Pour the batter into the prepared loaf pan and smooth the top with a spatula.
Bake in the preheated oven for 45-50 minutes, or until a toothpick inserted into the center of the cake comes out clean.
While the cake is baking, prepare the lemon drizzle.

**For the Drizzle:**

In a small saucepan, heat the lemon juice and granulated sugar over medium heat, stirring occasionally, until the sugar has dissolved and the mixture has slightly thickened. Remove from heat and set aside.

Assembling the Cake:

Once the cake is baked, remove it from the oven and place it on a wire rack. While the cake is still warm, poke several holes on top using a toothpick or skewer.
Slowly pour the lemon drizzle over the warm cake, allowing it to soak into the holes and drizzle down the sides.
Let the cake cool completely in the pan before removing it and slicing it.
Slice and serve your delicious lemon drizzle cake, and enjoy!

This lemon drizzle cake is perfect for tea time, dessert, or any time you're craving a bright and citrusy treat. It's sure to be a hit with family and friends!

## Carrot Cake with Cream Cheese Frosting

Ingredients:

For the Carrot Cake:

- 2 cups all-purpose flour
- 1 teaspoon baking powder
- 1 teaspoon baking soda
- 1/2 teaspoon salt
- 2 teaspoons ground cinnamon
- 1/2 teaspoon ground nutmeg
- 1/2 teaspoon ground ginger
- 1 cup granulated sugar
- 1 cup packed brown sugar
- 1 cup vegetable oil
- 4 large eggs, room temperature
- 2 teaspoons vanilla extract
- 3 cups grated carrots (about 3-4 medium carrots)
- 1 cup chopped nuts (optional)
- 1/2 cup raisins (optional)

For the Cream Cheese Frosting:

- 8 ounces cream cheese, softened
- 1/2 cup unsalted butter, softened
- 4 cups powdered sugar
- 1 teaspoon vanilla extract

Instructions:

For the Carrot Cake:

Preheat your oven to 350°F (175°C). Grease and flour two 9-inch round cake pans or one 9x13-inch rectangular cake pan.
In a large bowl, sift together the flour, baking powder, baking soda, salt, cinnamon, nutmeg, and ginger.
In another bowl, whisk together the granulated sugar, brown sugar, vegetable oil, eggs, and vanilla extract until well combined.

Gradually add the wet ingredients to the dry ingredients, mixing until just combined.

Fold in the grated carrots, chopped nuts (if using), and raisins (if using) until evenly distributed.

Pour the batter into the prepared cake pans, spreading it out evenly.

Bake in the preheated oven for 25-30 minutes for round cakes or 35-40 minutes for a rectangular cake, or until a toothpick inserted into the center comes out clean.

Remove the cakes from the oven and let them cool in the pans for 10 minutes. Then, transfer the cakes to a wire rack to cool completely before frosting.

For the Cream Cheese Frosting:

In a large bowl, beat the cream cheese and butter together until smooth and creamy.

Gradually add the powdered sugar, one cup at a time, beating well after each addition.

Stir in the vanilla extract and mix until smooth and creamy.

Assembling the Cake:

Once the cakes have cooled completely, place one cake layer on a serving plate or cake stand.

Spread a layer of cream cheese frosting evenly over the top of the first cake layer.

Place the second cake layer on top and spread the remaining frosting over the top and sides of the cake.

Optionally, decorate the cake with chopped nuts or grated carrots.

Refrigerate the cake for at least 1 hour before serving to allow the frosting to set.

Slice and serve your delicious carrot cake with cream cheese frosting, and enjoy!

This carrot cake is perfect for any occasion, from birthdays to potlucks, and it's sure to be a hit with family and friends.

**Banana Bread Cake**

Ingredients:

- 2 cups all-purpose flour
- 1 teaspoon baking powder
- 1/2 teaspoon baking soda
- 1/2 teaspoon salt
- 1 teaspoon ground cinnamon
- 1/2 cup unsalted butter, softened
- 3/4 cup granulated sugar
- 2 large eggs, room temperature
- 1 teaspoon vanilla extract
- 3 ripe bananas, mashed (about 1 1/2 cups)
- 1/3 cup sour cream or Greek yogurt
- Optional: 1/2 cup chopped nuts (such as walnuts or pecans)
- Optional: 1/2 cup chocolate chips

Instructions:

Preheat your oven to 350°F (175°C). Grease and flour a 9-inch round cake pan or line it with parchment paper for easier removal.

In a medium bowl, whisk together the flour, baking powder, baking soda, salt, and ground cinnamon. Set aside.

In a large mixing bowl, cream together the softened butter and granulated sugar until light and fluffy.

Beat in the eggs, one at a time, until well incorporated. Stir in the vanilla extract.

Add the mashed bananas to the wet ingredients and mix until combined.

Gradually add the dry ingredients to the wet ingredients, mixing until just combined. Be careful not to overmix.

Fold in the sour cream or Greek yogurt until evenly distributed. If using, gently fold in the chopped nuts and/or chocolate chips.

Pour the batter into the prepared cake pan, spreading it out evenly with a spatula.

Bake in the preheated oven for 35-40 minutes, or until a toothpick inserted into the center comes out clean.

Remove the cake from the oven and allow it to cool in the pan for 10 minutes before transferring it to a wire rack to cool completely.

Once cooled, you can optionally dust the top with powdered sugar or drizzle with a simple glaze made from powdered sugar and milk.

Slice and serve your delicious banana bread cake, and enjoy!

This banana bread cake is perfect for breakfast, brunch, or as a sweet treat any time of day. It's moist, flavorful, and sure to be a hit with banana bread lovers!

**Marble Cake**

Ingredients:

- 2 cups all-purpose flour
- 1 teaspoon baking powder
- 1/2 teaspoon baking soda
- 1/2 teaspoon salt
- 1/2 cup unsalted butter, softened
- 1 cup granulated sugar
- 2 large eggs, room temperature
- 2 teaspoons vanilla extract
- 1/2 cup milk
- 1/4 cup unsweetened cocoa powder
- 1/4 cup hot water

Instructions:

Preheat your oven to 350°F (175°C). Grease and flour a 9x5-inch loaf pan or two 9-inch round cake pans.

In a medium bowl, whisk together the flour, baking powder, baking soda, and salt. Set aside.

In a large mixing bowl, cream together the softened butter and granulated sugar until light and fluffy.

Beat in the eggs, one at a time, until well incorporated. Stir in the vanilla extract.

Gradually add the dry ingredients to the wet ingredients, alternating with the milk, beginning and ending with the dry ingredients. Mix until just combined. Be careful not to overmix.

In a small bowl, mix the cocoa powder and hot water until smooth to create the chocolate batter.

Pour half of the vanilla batter into another bowl. Add the chocolate batter to one of the bowls and mix until well combined.

Spoon dollops of the vanilla and chocolate batters alternately into the prepared pan(s).

Use a knife or a skewer to gently swirl the batters together to create a marbled pattern. Be careful not to overmix; you want distinct swirls.

Bake in the preheated oven for 40-45 minutes for a loaf pan or 25-30 minutes for round cake pans, or until a toothpick inserted into the center comes out clean.

Remove the cake from the oven and let it cool in the pan(s) for 10 minutes before transferring it to a wire rack to cool completely.

Once cooled, slice and serve your delicious marble cake.

Enjoy the rich combination of vanilla and chocolate flavors in this beautiful marble cake!

You can also dust the top with powdered sugar or drizzle with a glaze if desired.

**Coconut Cake**

Ingredients:

For the Cake:

- 2 1/2 cups all-purpose flour
- 2 1/2 teaspoons baking powder
- 1/2 teaspoon salt
- 1 cup unsalted butter, softened
- 1 1/2 cups granulated sugar
- 4 large eggs, room temperature
- 1 teaspoon vanilla extract
- 1 cup canned coconut milk (shake well before measuring)
- 1 cup sweetened shredded coconut

For the Coconut Frosting:

- 1 cup unsalted butter, softened
- 4 cups powdered sugar
- 1/4 cup canned coconut milk (shake well before measuring)
- 1 teaspoon vanilla extract
- 1 cup sweetened shredded coconut, for garnish

Instructions:

For the Cake:

Preheat your oven to 350°F (175°C). Grease and flour three 9-inch round cake pans.
In a medium bowl, sift together the flour, baking powder, and salt. Set aside.
In a large mixing bowl, cream together the softened butter and granulated sugar until light and fluffy.
Beat in the eggs, one at a time, until well incorporated. Stir in the vanilla extract.
Gradually add the dry ingredients to the wet ingredients, alternating with the coconut milk, beginning and ending with the dry ingredients. Mix until just combined.
Fold in the sweetened shredded coconut until evenly distributed throughout the batter.
Divide the batter evenly between the prepared cake pans.

Bake in the preheated oven for 25-30 minutes, or until a toothpick inserted into the center of the cakes comes out clean.

Remove the cakes from the oven and let them cool in the pans for 10 minutes before transferring them to a wire rack to cool completely.

For the Coconut Frosting:

In a large mixing bowl, beat the softened butter until smooth and creamy.

Gradually add the powdered sugar, one cup at a time, beating well after each addition.

Add the coconut milk and vanilla extract, and continue to beat until the frosting is smooth and creamy.

If the frosting is too thick, you can add more coconut milk, one tablespoon at a time, until you reach your desired consistency.

Assembling the Cake:

Once the cakes have cooled completely, place one cake layer on a serving plate or cake stand.

Spread a layer of frosting evenly over the top of the first cake layer.

Repeat with the remaining cake layers and frosting.

Use the remaining frosting to cover the top and sides of the cake.

Gently press sweetened shredded coconut onto the top and sides of the cake for garnish.

Refrigerate the cake for at least 30 minutes before slicing and serving to allow the frosting to set.

Enjoy the delicious tropical flavor of this homemade coconut cake! It's perfect for birthdays, celebrations, or any special occasion.

**Strawberry Shortcake**

Ingredients:

For the Shortcakes:

- 2 cups all-purpose flour
- 1/4 cup granulated sugar
- 1 tablespoon baking powder
- 1/2 teaspoon salt
- 1/2 cup unsalted butter, cold and cut into small pieces
- 2/3 cup milk
- 1 teaspoon vanilla extract
- 1 tablespoon heavy cream (for brushing)
- 1 tablespoon granulated sugar (for sprinkling)

For the Strawberry Filling:

- 1 1/2 pounds fresh strawberries, hulled and sliced
- 1/4 cup granulated sugar (adjust to taste)
- 1 teaspoon lemon juice
- Optional: Additional sliced strawberries for garnish

For the Whipped Cream:

- 1 cup heavy cream, chilled
- 2 tablespoons powdered sugar
- 1 teaspoon vanilla extract

Instructions:

For the Shortcakes:

Preheat your oven to 425°F (220°C). Line a baking sheet with parchment paper.
In a large bowl, whisk together the flour, sugar, baking powder, and salt.
Cut in the cold butter using a pastry cutter or fork until the mixture resembles coarse crumbs.
In a separate bowl, mix together the milk and vanilla extract. Gradually add the milk mixture to the flour mixture, stirring until just combined.
Turn the dough out onto a lightly floured surface and gently knead it a few times until it comes together.

Pat the dough into a circle about 1 inch thick. Use a round cookie cutter or a glass to cut out shortcakes. Place the shortcakes on the prepared baking sheet. Brush the tops of the shortcakes with heavy cream and sprinkle with granulated sugar.

Bake in the preheated oven for 12-15 minutes, or until golden brown. Remove from the oven and let cool slightly before assembling the shortcakes.

For the Strawberry Filling:

In a large bowl, combine the sliced strawberries, granulated sugar, and lemon juice. Stir gently to coat the strawberries evenly in the sugar.

Let the strawberries sit at room temperature for about 15-20 minutes to macerate, releasing their juices and becoming sweeter.

For the Whipped Cream:

In a chilled mixing bowl, beat the heavy cream, powdered sugar, and vanilla extract with an electric mixer on high speed until stiff peaks form.

Assembling the Strawberry Shortcakes:

Slice the cooled shortcakes in half horizontally.
Place the bottom halves of the shortcakes on serving plates.
Spoon a generous amount of the macerated strawberries onto each shortcake bottom.
Top with a dollop of whipped cream.
Place the top halves of the shortcakes over the whipped cream.
Garnish with additional sliced strawberries, if desired.
Serve immediately and enjoy your delicious strawberry shortcakes!

Strawberry shortcakes are best enjoyed fresh, so assemble them just before serving. They're a perfect dessert for summer gatherings, picnics, or any time you're craving a sweet treat!

**Black Forest Cake**

Ingredients:

For the Chocolate Cake Layers:

- 1 3/4 cups all-purpose flour
- 3/4 cup unsweetened cocoa powder
- 2 cups granulated sugar
- 1 1/2 teaspoons baking powder
- 1 1/2 teaspoons baking soda
- 1 teaspoon salt
- 2 large eggs, room temperature
- 1 cup milk
- 1/2 cup vegetable oil
- 2 teaspoons vanilla extract
- 1 cup boiling water

For the Cherry Filling:

- 3 cups pitted cherries (fresh or canned), drained
- 1/4 cup granulated sugar
- 2 tablespoons cornstarch
- 1 tablespoon lemon juice
- 1/4 cup cherry liqueur (Kirsch), optional

For the Whipped Cream Frosting:

- 3 cups heavy cream, chilled
- 1/2 cup powdered sugar
- 1 teaspoon vanilla extract

For Garnish:

- Chocolate shavings or curls
- Maraschino cherries

Instructions:

For the Chocolate Cake Layers:

Preheat your oven to 350°F (175°C). Grease and flour two 9-inch round cake pans.

In a large mixing bowl, sift together the flour, cocoa powder, sugar, baking powder, baking soda, and salt.

Add the eggs, milk, oil, and vanilla extract to the dry ingredients. Beat on medium speed for 2 minutes.

Stir in the boiling water until the batter is well combined (it will be thin).

Pour the batter evenly into the prepared cake pans.

Bake in the preheated oven for 30-35 minutes, or until a toothpick inserted into the center of the cakes comes out clean.

Remove the cakes from the oven and let them cool in the pans for 10 minutes before transferring them to a wire rack to cool completely.

For the Cherry Filling:

In a saucepan, combine the pitted cherries, sugar, cornstarch, and lemon juice. Cook over medium heat, stirring constantly, until the mixture thickens and the cherries soften, about 5-7 minutes.

Remove from heat and stir in the cherry liqueur, if using. Allow the filling to cool completely.

For the Whipped Cream Frosting:

In a chilled mixing bowl, beat the heavy cream, powdered sugar, and vanilla extract until stiff peaks form.

Assembling the Black Forest Cake:

Place one chocolate cake layer on a serving plate or cake stand.

Spread a layer of whipped cream frosting over the top of the cake layer.

Spoon half of the cherry filling over the whipped cream frosting.

Place the second chocolate cake layer on top and press down gently.

Spread the remaining whipped cream frosting over the top and sides of the cake.

Spoon the remaining cherry filling over the top of the cake.

Garnish with chocolate shavings or curls and maraschino cherries.

Refrigerate the cake for at least 1 hour before slicing and serving to allow the flavors to meld together.

Enjoy the rich chocolatey layers, creamy whipped cream frosting, and tart cherries of this decadent Black Forest Cake! It's a perfect dessert for special occasions or celebrations.

**Pineapple Upside-Down Cake**

Ingredients:

For the topping:

- 1/4 cup unsalted butter
- 3/4 cup packed brown sugar
- 7-8 canned pineapple rings
- Maraschino cherries (optional), for garnish

For the cake batter:

- 1 1/2 cups all-purpose flour
- 1 1/2 teaspoons baking powder
- 1/4 teaspoon salt
- 1/2 cup unsalted butter, softened
- 1 cup granulated sugar
- 2 large eggs
- 1 teaspoon vanilla extract
- 1/2 cup pineapple juice (reserved from the canned pineapple)

Instructions:

Preheat your oven to 350°F (175°C). Grease a 9-inch round cake pan and line the bottom with parchment paper.
In a small saucepan, melt the butter over low heat. Once melted, pour it into the prepared cake pan and spread it evenly over the bottom.
Sprinkle the brown sugar evenly over the melted butter in the cake pan.
Arrange the pineapple rings on top of the brown sugar. You can also place a maraschino cherry in the center of each pineapple ring if desired.
In a medium bowl, whisk together the flour, baking powder, and salt. Set aside.
In a large mixing bowl, cream together the softened butter and granulated sugar until light and fluffy.
Beat in the eggs, one at a time, until well combined. Stir in the vanilla extract.
Gradually add the dry ingredients to the wet ingredients, alternating with the pineapple juice, beginning and ending with the dry ingredients. Mix until just combined.
Pour the cake batter over the arranged pineapple slices in the cake pan, spreading it out evenly.

Bake in the preheated oven for 40-45 minutes, or until a toothpick inserted into the center comes out clean.

Remove the cake from the oven and let it cool in the pan for 10 minutes.

Run a knife around the edges of the cake to loosen it from the pan, then carefully invert it onto a serving plate.

Allow the cake to cool slightly before serving. Serve slices warm or at room temperature.

Enjoy the sweet and tangy flavors of this classic Pineapple Upside-Down Cake! It's perfect for dessert or even as a sweet treat with coffee or tea.

**Funfetti Cake**

Ingredients:

For the Cake:

- 2 1/2 cups all-purpose flour
- 2 1/2 teaspoons baking powder
- 1/2 teaspoon salt
- 1 cup unsalted butter, softened
- 1 3/4 cups granulated sugar
- 4 large eggs, room temperature
- 1 tablespoon vanilla extract
- 1 cup whole milk, room temperature
- 1/2 cup rainbow sprinkles (jimmies)

For the Frosting:

- 1 cup unsalted butter, softened
- 4 cups powdered sugar
- 2-3 tablespoons whole milk or heavy cream
- 1 teaspoon vanilla extract
- Additional rainbow sprinkles for decorating

Instructions:

For the Cake:

Preheat your oven to 350°F (175°C). Grease and flour three 8-inch round cake pans or two 9-inch round cake pans.
In a medium bowl, whisk together the flour, baking powder, and salt. Set aside.
In a large mixing bowl, cream together the softened butter and granulated sugar until light and fluffy.
Beat in the eggs, one at a time, until well combined. Stir in the vanilla extract.
Gradually add the dry ingredients to the wet ingredients, alternating with the milk, beginning and ending with the dry ingredients. Mix until just combined.
Gently fold in the rainbow sprinkles until evenly distributed throughout the batter.
Divide the batter evenly between the prepared cake pans.
Bake in the preheated oven for 25-30 minutes, or until a toothpick inserted into the center of the cakes comes out clean.

Remove the cakes from the oven and let them cool in the pans for 10 minutes before transferring them to a wire rack to cool completely.

For the Frosting:

In a large mixing bowl, beat the softened butter until smooth and creamy. Gradually add the powdered sugar, one cup at a time, beating well after each addition.

Add the vanilla extract and 2 tablespoons of milk or cream. Beat until smooth and creamy. If the frosting is too thick, add an additional tablespoon of milk or cream until you reach your desired consistency.

Assembling the Cake:

Once the cakes have cooled completely, place one cake layer on a serving plate or cake stand.
Spread a layer of frosting evenly over the top of the first cake layer.
Repeat with the remaining cake layers and frosting.
Use the remaining frosting to cover the top and sides of the cake.
Decorate the cake with additional rainbow sprinkles.
Slice and serve your delicious Funfetti cake!

Enjoy this colorful and whimsical Funfetti cake for birthdays, parties, or any special occasion! It's sure to bring joy to everyone who tastes it.

**Almond Cake**

Ingredients:

- 1 cup unsalted butter, softened
- 1 cup granulated sugar
- 4 large eggs, room temperature
- 1 teaspoon almond extract
- 1 cup all-purpose flour
- 1 cup almond flour (ground almonds)
- 1 teaspoon baking powder
- 1/4 teaspoon salt
- 1/2 cup milk
- Sliced almonds, for garnish (optional)
- Powdered sugar, for dusting (optional)

Instructions:

Preheat your oven to 350°F (175°C). Grease and flour a 9-inch round cake pan or line it with parchment paper for easier removal.
In a large mixing bowl, cream together the softened butter and granulated sugar until light and fluffy.
Beat in the eggs, one at a time, until well incorporated. Stir in the almond extract.
In a separate bowl, whisk together the all-purpose flour, almond flour, baking powder, and salt.
Gradually add the dry ingredients to the wet ingredients, alternating with the milk, beginning and ending with the dry ingredients. Mix until just combined. Be careful not to overmix.
Pour the batter into the prepared cake pan, spreading it out evenly.
If desired, sprinkle sliced almonds over the top of the batter for garnish.
Bake in the preheated oven for 30-35 minutes, or until a toothpick inserted into the center comes out clean.
Remove the cake from the oven and let it cool in the pan for 10 minutes before transferring it to a wire rack to cool completely.
Once cooled, you can optionally dust the top of the cake with powdered sugar for decoration.
Slice and serve your delicious almond cake, and enjoy!

This almond cake is perfect for any occasion, from afternoon tea to dessert after a special meal. Its delicate almond flavor and moist texture are sure to be a hit with family and friends.

**Tiramisu Cake**

Ingredients:

For the Cake Layers:

- 2 cups all-purpose flour
- 2 teaspoons baking powder
- 1/2 teaspoon baking soda
- 1/2 teaspoon salt
- 1/2 cup unsalted butter, softened
- 1 cup granulated sugar
- 2 large eggs, room temperature
- 1 teaspoon vanilla extract
- 1 cup buttermilk, room temperature

For the Coffee Soaking Syrup:

- 1 cup strong brewed coffee, cooled
- 1/4 cup granulated sugar
- 2 tablespoons coffee liqueur (optional)

For the Mascarpone Filling:

- 16 ounces mascarpone cheese, softened
- 1 cup powdered sugar
- 1 teaspoon vanilla extract

For Assembly and Decoration:

- Cocoa powder, for dusting
- Chocolate shavings, for garnish
- Ladyfinger cookies, for decoration

Instructions:

For the Cake Layers:

Preheat your oven to 350°F (175°C). Grease and flour two 9-inch round cake pans.

In a medium bowl, whisk together the flour, baking powder, baking soda, and salt. Set aside.

In a large mixing bowl, cream together the softened butter and granulated sugar until light and fluffy.

Beat in the eggs, one at a time, until well incorporated. Stir in the vanilla extract.

Gradually add the dry ingredients to the wet ingredients, alternating with the buttermilk, beginning and ending with the dry ingredients. Mix until just combined.

Divide the batter evenly between the prepared cake pans.

Bake in the preheated oven for 25-30 minutes, or until a toothpick inserted into the center comes out clean.

Remove the cakes from the oven and let them cool in the pans for 10 minutes before transferring them to a wire rack to cool completely.

For the Coffee Soaking Syrup:

In a small saucepan, combine the strong brewed coffee and granulated sugar. Heat over medium heat, stirring occasionally, until the sugar is dissolved.

Remove the saucepan from the heat and stir in the coffee liqueur (if using). Let the syrup cool completely before using.

For the Mascarpone Filling:

In a large mixing bowl, beat the softened mascarpone cheese until smooth and creamy.

Gradually add the powdered sugar and vanilla extract, beating until well combined and smooth.

For Assembly:

Once the cake layers have cooled completely, use a serrated knife to level the tops of the cakes if necessary.

Place one cake layer on a serving plate or cake stand. Using a pastry brush, generously brush the top of the cake layer with the coffee soaking syrup.

Spread a layer of mascarpone filling over the soaked cake layer.

Place the second cake layer on top and repeat the process, brushing the top with the coffee soaking syrup and spreading another layer of mascarpone filling.

Dust the top of the cake with cocoa powder and garnish with chocolate shavings.

Optionally, arrange ladyfinger cookies around the sides of the cake for decoration.
Refrigerate the tiramisu cake for at least 2 hours before serving to allow the flavors to meld and the cake to set.

Enjoy the decadent flavors of this homemade tiramisu cake! It's perfect for special occasions or any time you're craving a luxurious dessert.

**Peanut Butter Chocolate Cake**

Ingredients:

For the Chocolate Cake Layers:

- 2 cups all-purpose flour
- 1 cup unsweetened cocoa powder
- 2 cups granulated sugar
- 2 teaspoons baking powder
- 1 teaspoon baking soda
- 1 teaspoon salt
- 2 large eggs, room temperature
- 1 cup buttermilk, room temperature
- 1 cup hot water
- 1/2 cup vegetable oil
- 2 teaspoons vanilla extract

For the Peanut Butter Frosting:

- 1 cup unsalted butter, softened
- 1 cup creamy peanut butter
- 4 cups powdered sugar
- 1 teaspoon vanilla extract
- 1/4 cup heavy cream or milk (if needed for consistency)

For Assembly and Decoration:

- Chocolate ganache (optional, for drizzling)
- Chopped peanuts (optional, for garnish)

Instructions:

For the Chocolate Cake Layers:

Preheat your oven to 350°F (175°C). Grease and flour three 9-inch round cake pans.

In a large mixing bowl, sift together the flour, cocoa powder, granulated sugar, baking powder, baking soda, and salt.

In a separate bowl, whisk together the eggs, buttermilk, hot water, vegetable oil, and vanilla extract until well combined.

Gradually add the wet ingredients to the dry ingredients, mixing until smooth and well combined.

Divide the batter evenly between the prepared cake pans.

Bake in the preheated oven for 25-30 minutes, or until a toothpick inserted into the center of the cakes comes out clean.

Remove the cakes from the oven and let them cool in the pans for 10 minutes before transferring them to a wire rack to cool completely.

For the Peanut Butter Frosting:

In a large mixing bowl, beat together the softened butter and creamy peanut butter until smooth and creamy.

Gradually add the powdered sugar, one cup at a time, beating well after each addition.

Stir in the vanilla extract.

If the frosting is too thick, you can add heavy cream or milk, one tablespoon at a time, until you reach your desired consistency.

For Assembly:

Once the cake layers have cooled completely, place one cake layer on a serving plate or cake stand.

Spread a layer of peanut butter frosting evenly over the top of the cake layer.

Repeat with the remaining cake layers and frosting.

Optionally, drizzle chocolate ganache over the top of the cake and sprinkle chopped peanuts for garnish.

Refrigerate the cake for at least 30 minutes before slicing and serving to allow the frosting to set.

Enjoy the irresistible combination of peanut butter and chocolate in this homemade cake! It's perfect for birthdays, celebrations, or any time you're craving a decadent dessert.

**Coffee Cake**

Ingredients:

For the Cake:

- 2 cups all-purpose flour
- 1 cup granulated sugar
- 1/2 cup unsalted butter, softened
- 2 large eggs, room temperature
- 1 cup sour cream
- 1 teaspoon vanilla extract
- 1 teaspoon baking powder
- 1/2 teaspoon baking soda
- 1/4 teaspoon salt

For the Streusel Topping:

- 1/2 cup all-purpose flour
- 1/2 cup packed brown sugar
- 1/4 cup unsalted butter, softened
- 1 teaspoon ground cinnamon
- 1/4 cup chopped nuts (optional)

Instructions:

Preheat your oven to 350°F (175°C). Grease and flour a 9x9-inch square baking pan or a 9-inch round cake pan.

In a large mixing bowl, cream together the softened butter and granulated sugar until light and fluffy.

Beat in the eggs, one at a time, until well incorporated. Stir in the sour cream and vanilla extract.

In a separate bowl, sift together the flour, baking powder, baking soda, and salt. Gradually add the dry ingredients to the wet ingredients, mixing until just combined. Be careful not to overmix.

Spread the cake batter evenly into the prepared baking pan.

In a small bowl, combine all the streusel topping ingredients (flour, brown sugar, softened butter, cinnamon, and chopped nuts if using). Mix with a fork or your fingers until crumbly.

Sprinkle the streusel topping evenly over the cake batter in the pan.

Bake in the preheated oven for 35-40 minutes, or until a toothpick inserted into the center comes out clean.

Remove the coffee cake from the oven and let it cool in the pan for 10 minutes before transferring it to a wire rack to cool completely.

Once cooled, slice and serve your delicious coffee cake. Enjoy with a hot cup of coffee or tea!

This coffee cake is perfect for breakfast, brunch, or as a sweet treat any time of day. Its moist and tender crumb, paired with the crunchy streusel topping, makes it a delightful indulgence.

**Apple Spice Cake**

Ingredients:

For the Cake:

- 2 cups all-purpose flour
- 1 teaspoon baking powder
- 1/2 teaspoon baking soda
- 1/2 teaspoon salt
- 1 teaspoon ground cinnamon
- 1/2 teaspoon ground nutmeg
- 1/4 teaspoon ground cloves
- 1/2 cup unsalted butter, softened
- 1 cup granulated sugar
- 2 large eggs, room temperature
- 1 teaspoon vanilla extract
- 1 cup unsweetened applesauce
- 1 cup grated apples (such as Granny Smith)
- 1/2 cup chopped walnuts or pecans (optional)

For the Cream Cheese Frosting:

- 8 ounces cream cheese, softened
- 1/2 cup unsalted butter, softened
- 4 cups powdered sugar
- 1 teaspoon vanilla extract

Instructions:

For the Cake:

Preheat your oven to 350°F (175°C). Grease and flour a 9x13-inch baking pan or two 9-inch round cake pans.
In a medium bowl, whisk together the flour, baking powder, baking soda, salt, cinnamon, nutmeg, and cloves. Set aside.
In a large mixing bowl, cream together the softened butter and granulated sugar until light and fluffy.
Beat in the eggs, one at a time, until well incorporated. Stir in the vanilla extract.
Gradually add the dry ingredients to the wet ingredients, mixing until just combined.

Fold in the unsweetened applesauce, grated apples, and chopped nuts (if using) until evenly distributed throughout the batter.

Pour the batter into the prepared baking pan(s), spreading it out evenly.

Bake in the preheated oven for 30-35 minutes for a 9x13-inch pan or 25-30 minutes for round cake pans, or until a toothpick inserted into the center comes out clean.

Remove the cake from the oven and let it cool in the pan(s) for 10 minutes before transferring it to a wire rack to cool completely.

For the Cream Cheese Frosting:

In a large mixing bowl, beat the softened cream cheese and butter together until smooth and creamy.

Gradually add the powdered sugar, one cup at a time, beating well after each addition.

Stir in the vanilla extract and mix until smooth and creamy.

Assembling the Cake:

Once the cake has cooled completely, spread a layer of cream cheese frosting over the top of the cake if using a single layer, or between the layers and on top if using two layers.

Optionally, garnish with additional chopped nuts or grated apple.

Slice and serve your delicious apple spice cake, and enjoy!

This apple spice cake is perfect for fall gatherings, holidays, or any time you're craving a cozy and comforting dessert.

**Pistachio Cake**

Ingredients:

For the Cake:

- 1 box (18.25 ounces) white or yellow cake mix
- 1 package (3.4 ounces) instant pistachio pudding mix
- 1 cup milk
- 1/2 cup vegetable oil
- 4 large eggs
- 1/2 cup chopped pistachios (optional, for added texture and flavor)

For the Frosting:

- 1 package (3.4 ounces) instant pistachio pudding mix
- 1 1/2 cups milk
- 1 package (8 ounces) cream cheese, softened
- 1/2 cup powdered sugar
- 1 container (8 ounces) frozen whipped topping, thawed
- Additional chopped pistachios, for garnish (optional)

Instructions:

For the Cake:

Preheat your oven to 350°F (175°C). Grease and flour a 9x13-inch baking pan or two 9-inch round cake pans.
In a large mixing bowl, combine the cake mix, pistachio pudding mix, milk, vegetable oil, and eggs. Beat on medium speed for 2 minutes, until well combined and smooth.
Fold in the chopped pistachios if using.
Pour the batter into the prepared baking pan(s), spreading it out evenly.
Bake in the preheated oven for 25-30 minutes for a 9x13-inch pan or 20-25 minutes for round cake pans, or until a toothpick inserted into the center comes out clean.
Remove the cake from the oven and let it cool completely in the pan(s) on a wire rack.

For the Frosting:

In a medium bowl, whisk together the instant pistachio pudding mix and milk until smooth. Let it set for about 5 minutes.

In another mixing bowl, beat the softened cream cheese and powdered sugar together until smooth and creamy.

Gradually add the prepared pistachio pudding to the cream cheese mixture, beating until well combined.

Gently fold in the thawed whipped topping until smooth and creamy.

Assembling the Cake:

If using two round cake layers, level the tops of the cakes if necessary.

Place one cake layer on a serving plate or cake stand. Spread a layer of frosting over the top.

Place the second cake layer on top and spread the remaining frosting over the top and sides of the cake.

Optionally, garnish with additional chopped pistachios.

Refrigerate the cake for at least 1 hour before serving to allow the frosting to set.

Slice and serve your delicious pistachio cake, and enjoy!

This pistachio cake is perfect for any occasion, from birthdays to potlucks, and it's sure to be a hit with its unique flavor and beautiful green color.

**Honey Lavender Cake**

Ingredients:

For the Cake:

- 2 cups all-purpose flour
- 2 teaspoons baking powder
- 1/2 teaspoon baking soda
- 1/2 teaspoon salt
- 1/2 cup unsalted butter, softened
- 3/4 cup granulated sugar
- 2 large eggs, room temperature
- 1/4 cup honey
- 1 tablespoon culinary lavender buds, finely chopped
- 1 cup buttermilk, room temperature
- 1 teaspoon vanilla extract

For the Honey Lavender Buttercream Frosting:

- 1 cup unsalted butter, softened
- 4 cups powdered sugar
- 2 tablespoons honey
- 1 tablespoon culinary lavender buds, finely chopped
- 2-3 tablespoons milk or cream
- Purple food coloring (optional)
- Additional culinary lavender buds, for garnish (optional)

Instructions:

For the Cake:

Preheat your oven to 350°F (175°C). Grease and flour two 9-inch round cake pans.

In a medium bowl, whisk together the flour, baking powder, baking soda, and salt. Set aside.

In a large mixing bowl, cream together the softened butter and granulated sugar until light and fluffy.

Beat in the eggs, one at a time, until well incorporated. Stir in the honey and finely chopped culinary lavender buds.

Gradually add the dry ingredients to the wet ingredients, alternating with the buttermilk, beginning and ending with the dry ingredients. Mix until just combined.

Stir in the vanilla extract until evenly distributed throughout the batter.

Divide the batter evenly between the prepared cake pans.

Bake in the preheated oven for 25-30 minutes, or until a toothpick inserted into the center comes out clean.

Remove the cakes from the oven and let them cool in the pans for 10 minutes before transferring them to a wire rack to cool completely.

For the Honey Lavender Buttercream Frosting:

In a large mixing bowl, beat the softened butter until smooth and creamy.

Gradually add the powdered sugar, one cup at a time, beating well after each addition.

Beat in the honey and finely chopped culinary lavender buds until well combined.

Add milk or cream, one tablespoon at a time, until you reach your desired consistency.

If desired, add a few drops of purple food coloring to achieve a lavender hue.

Assembling the Cake:

Once the cakes have cooled completely, place one cake layer on a serving plate or cake stand.

Spread a layer of honey lavender buttercream frosting evenly over the top of the first cake layer.

Place the second cake layer on top and spread the remaining frosting over the top and sides of the cake.

Optionally, garnish with additional culinary lavender buds for decoration.

Slice and serve your delicious honey lavender cake, and enjoy!

This honey lavender cake is perfect for special occasions or any time you want to indulge in a unique and elegant dessert. The combination of floral lavender and sweet honey is sure to impress your guests.

**Orange Creamsicle Cake**

Ingredients:

For the Cake:

- 2 cups all-purpose flour
- 1 1/2 teaspoons baking powder
- 1/2 teaspoon baking soda
- 1/2 teaspoon salt
- 1/2 cup unsalted butter, softened
- 1 cup granulated sugar
- 2 large eggs, room temperature
- 1 teaspoon vanilla extract
- 1 tablespoon orange zest
- 3/4 cup freshly squeezed orange juice
- 1/4 cup buttermilk

For the Creamsicle Frosting:

- 1/2 cup unsalted butter, softened
- 8 ounces cream cheese, softened
- 4 cups powdered sugar
- 1 teaspoon vanilla extract
- 2 tablespoons freshly squeezed orange juice
- 1 tablespoon orange zest
- Orange food coloring (optional)

Instructions:

For the Cake:

Preheat your oven to 350°F (175°C). Grease and flour two 9-inch round cake pans.

In a medium bowl, whisk together the flour, baking powder, baking soda, and salt. Set aside.

In a large mixing bowl, cream together the softened butter and granulated sugar until light and fluffy.

Beat in the eggs, one at a time, until well incorporated. Stir in the vanilla extract and orange zest.

Gradually add the dry ingredients to the wet ingredients, alternating with the orange juice and buttermilk, beginning and ending with the dry ingredients. Mix until just combined.

Divide the batter evenly between the prepared cake pans.

Bake in the preheated oven for 25-30 minutes, or until a toothpick inserted into the center comes out clean.

Remove the cakes from the oven and let them cool in the pans for 10 minutes before transferring them to a wire rack to cool completely.

For the Creamsicle Frosting:

In a large mixing bowl, beat the softened butter and cream cheese together until smooth and creamy.

Gradually add the powdered sugar, one cup at a time, beating well after each addition.

Beat in the vanilla extract, freshly squeezed orange juice, and orange zest until well combined.

If desired, add a few drops of orange food coloring to achieve a creamsicle hue.

Assembling the Cake:

Once the cakes have cooled completely, place one cake layer on a serving plate or cake stand.

Spread a layer of creamsicle frosting evenly over the top of the first cake layer.

Place the second cake layer on top and spread the remaining frosting over the top and sides of the cake.

Optionally, garnish with additional orange zest or orange slices for decoration.

Slice and serve your delicious orange creamsicle cake, and enjoy!

This orange creamsicle cake is perfect for summer gatherings, birthdays, or any time you're craving a refreshing and nostalgic dessert. The combination of tangy orange and creamy vanilla is sure to delight your taste buds.

**Raspberry Swirl Cake**

Ingredients:

For the Cake:

- 1 1/2 cups all-purpose flour
- 1 1/2 teaspoons baking powder
- 1/2 teaspoon baking soda
- 1/4 teaspoon salt
- 1/2 cup unsalted butter, softened
- 3/4 cup granulated sugar
- 2 large eggs, room temperature
- 1 teaspoon vanilla extract
- 1/2 cup sour cream
- 1/2 cup milk

For the Raspberry Swirl:

- 1 cup fresh or frozen raspberries
- 2 tablespoons granulated sugar
- 1 tablespoon lemon juice

Instructions:

For the Cake:

Preheat your oven to 350°F (175°C). Grease and flour a 9-inch round cake pan or line it with parchment paper for easier removal.
In a medium bowl, whisk together the flour, baking powder, baking soda, and salt. Set aside.
In a large mixing bowl, cream together the softened butter and granulated sugar until light and fluffy.
Beat in the eggs, one at a time, until well incorporated. Stir in the vanilla extract.
Gradually add the dry ingredients to the wet ingredients, alternating with the sour cream and milk, beginning and ending with the dry ingredients. Mix until just combined.
Pour the batter into the prepared cake pan, spreading it out evenly.

For the Raspberry Swirl:

In a small saucepan, combine the raspberries, granulated sugar, and lemon juice.

Cook over medium heat, stirring occasionally, until the raspberries break down and the mixture thickens, about 5-7 minutes.

Remove the saucepan from the heat and strain the raspberry mixture through a fine-mesh sieve to remove the seeds. You should have about 1/2 cup of raspberry puree.

Allow the raspberry puree to cool slightly.

Assembling the Cake:

Once the raspberry puree has cooled slightly, spoon dollops of it onto the surface of the cake batter in the pan.

Use a knife or skewer to gently swirl the raspberry puree into the cake batter to create a marbled effect.

Bake the cake in the preheated oven for 25-30 minutes, or until a toothpick inserted into the center comes out clean.

Remove the cake from the oven and let it cool in the pan for 10 minutes before transferring it to a wire rack to cool completely.

Once cooled, slice and serve your delicious raspberry swirl cake, and enjoy!

This raspberry swirl cake is perfect for any occasion, from brunch to dessert after a special meal. Its beautiful marbled appearance and burst of raspberry flavor make it a delightful treat for raspberry lovers!

**Blueberry Lemon Cake**

Ingredients:

- 1 1/2 cups all-purpose flour
- 1 1/2 teaspoons baking powder
- 1/2 teaspoon salt
- 1/2 cup unsalted butter, softened
- 1 cup granulated sugar
- 2 large eggs
- 1 teaspoon vanilla extract
- 1 tablespoon lemon zest (from about 2 lemons)
- 1/2 cup milk
- 1 1/2 cups fresh blueberries

For the Lemon Glaze:

- 1 cup powdered sugar
- 2-3 tablespoons fresh lemon juice

Instructions:

Preheat Oven and Prepare Pan:
- Preheat your oven to 350°F (175°C). Grease and flour a 9-inch round cake pan or line it with parchment paper.

Mix Dry Ingredients:
- In a medium bowl, whisk together the flour, baking powder, and salt. Set aside.

Cream Butter and Sugar:
- In a large mixing bowl, cream together the softened butter and granulated sugar until light and fluffy.

Add Eggs and Flavorings:
- Beat in the eggs, one at a time, followed by the vanilla extract and lemon zest. Mix until well combined.

Alternate Adding Dry Ingredients and Milk:
- Gradually add the dry ingredients to the wet mixture, alternating with the milk. Begin and end with the dry ingredients, mixing until just combined. Be careful not to overmix.

Fold in Blueberries:

- Gently fold the fresh blueberries into the batter, being careful not to crush them.

Bake:
- Pour the batter into the prepared cake pan and spread it evenly. Bake in the preheated oven for 30-35 minutes, or until a toothpick inserted into the center comes out clean.

Cool:
- Allow the cake to cool in the pan for about 10 minutes before transferring it to a wire rack to cool completely.

Prepare Lemon Glaze:
- In a small bowl, whisk together the powdered sugar and fresh lemon juice until smooth. Adjust the consistency by adding more powdered sugar or lemon juice as needed.

Glaze the Cake:
- Once the cake has cooled, drizzle the lemon glaze over the top of the cake. You can also sprinkle additional lemon zest or blueberries on top for decoration, if desired.

Serve:
- Slice the cake and serve. Enjoy the delicious combination of flavors!

This blueberry lemon cake is perfect for any occasion, whether it's a special celebration or just a casual dessert. It's moist, flavorful, and sure to be a hit with friends and family!

**Mocha Espresso Cake**

Ingredients:

For the Cake:

- 1 3/4 cups all-purpose flour
- 3/4 cup unsweetened cocoa powder
- 1 3/4 cups granulated sugar
- 2 teaspoons baking powder
- 1 teaspoon baking soda
- 1/2 teaspoon salt
- 2 large eggs
- 1 cup milk
- 1/2 cup vegetable oil
- 2 teaspoons vanilla extract
- 1 cup hot brewed espresso or strong coffee, cooled to room temperature

For the Espresso Buttercream Frosting:

- 1 cup unsalted butter, softened
- 3-4 cups powdered sugar
- 2-3 tablespoons strong brewed espresso or coffee, cooled to room temperature
- 1 teaspoon vanilla extract

Optional Garnish:

- Chocolate shavings or cocoa powder for dusting

Instructions:

Preheat Oven and Prepare Pans:
- Preheat your oven to 350°F (175°C). Grease and flour two 9-inch round cake pans or line them with parchment paper.

Mix Dry Ingredients:
- In a large mixing bowl, sift together the flour, cocoa powder, sugar, baking powder, baking soda, and salt. Whisk until well combined.

Combine Wet Ingredients:
- In a separate bowl, whisk together the eggs, milk, vegetable oil, and vanilla extract until smooth.

Combine Wet and Dry Ingredients:
- Gradually add the wet ingredients to the dry ingredients, mixing until just combined. Be careful not to overmix.

Add Espresso:
- Stir in the brewed espresso or coffee until the batter is smooth and well combined.

Bake:
- Divide the batter evenly between the prepared cake pans. Bake in the preheated oven for 25-30 minutes, or until a toothpick inserted into the center comes out clean.

Cool:
- Allow the cakes to cool in the pans for 10 minutes, then transfer them to a wire rack to cool completely.

Prepare Espresso Buttercream Frosting:
- In a large mixing bowl, beat the softened butter until creamy. Gradually add the powdered sugar, 1 cup at a time, until the frosting reaches your desired consistency.
- Beat in the brewed espresso or coffee and vanilla extract until smooth and fluffy.

Assemble the Cake:
- Once the cakes have cooled completely, place one layer on a serving plate or cake stand. Spread a layer of espresso buttercream frosting over the top.
- Place the second cake layer on top and frost the top and sides of the cake with the remaining frosting.

Garnish (Optional):
- Garnish the cake with chocolate shavings or dust with cocoa powder for an elegant finishing touch.

Serve:
- Slice the cake and serve. Enjoy the rich, indulgent flavors of mocha espresso cake!

This decadent cake is perfect for special occasions or whenever you're craving a luxurious treat. The combination of chocolate and coffee creates a flavor sensation that's sure to impress!

**Salted Caramel Cake**

Ingredients:

For the Cake:

- 2 cups all-purpose flour
- 1 1/2 teaspoons baking powder
- 1/2 teaspoon baking soda
- 1/2 teaspoon salt
- 1/2 cup unsalted butter, softened
- 1 cup granulated sugar
- 2 large eggs
- 1 teaspoon vanilla extract
- 3/4 cup buttermilk

For the Salted Caramel Sauce:

- 1 cup granulated sugar
- 6 tablespoons unsalted butter, cut into pieces
- 1/2 cup heavy cream
- 1 teaspoon sea salt (or to taste)

For the Salted Caramel Buttercream Frosting:

- 1 cup unsalted butter, softened
- 4 cups powdered sugar
- 1/2 cup salted caramel sauce (cooled to room temperature)
- 1-2 tablespoons heavy cream (if needed)
- Sea salt, for sprinkling

Instructions:

Preheat Oven and Prepare Pans:
- Preheat your oven to 350°F (175°C). Grease and flour two 9-inch round cake pans or line them with parchment paper.

Mix Dry Ingredients:
- In a medium bowl, whisk together the flour, baking powder, baking soda, and salt. Set aside.

**Cream Butter and Sugar:**
- In a large mixing bowl, cream together the softened butter and granulated sugar until light and fluffy.

**Add Eggs and Vanilla:**
- Beat in the eggs, one at a time, followed by the vanilla extract, until well combined.

**Alternate Adding Dry Ingredients and Buttermilk:**
- Gradually add the dry ingredients to the wet mixture, alternating with the buttermilk. Begin and end with the dry ingredients, mixing until just combined. Be careful not to overmix.

**Divide Batter and Bake:**
- Divide the batter evenly between the prepared cake pans. Smooth the tops with a spatula. Bake in the preheated oven for 25-30 minutes, or until a toothpick inserted into the center comes out clean.

**Cool:**
- Allow the cakes to cool in the pans for 10 minutes, then transfer them to a wire rack to cool completely.

**Make Salted Caramel Sauce:**
- In a saucepan over medium heat, melt the granulated sugar, stirring constantly until it becomes a golden brown caramel. Be careful not to burn it.
- Once the sugar has melted and turned amber in color, add the butter and stir until melted and well combined.
- Slowly pour in the heavy cream while stirring continuously. Be cautious as the mixture will bubble up.
- Remove the caramel from heat and stir in the sea salt. Allow it to cool to room temperature.

**Prepare Salted Caramel Buttercream Frosting:**
- In a large mixing bowl, beat the softened butter until creamy. Gradually add the powdered sugar, 1 cup at a time, until smooth.
- Beat in the salted caramel sauce until well combined. If the frosting is too thick, you can add 1-2 tablespoons of heavy cream to reach your desired consistency.

**Assemble the Cake:**
- Once the cakes have cooled completely, place one layer on a serving plate or cake stand. Spread a layer of salted caramel buttercream frosting over the top.
- Place the second cake layer on top and frost the top and sides of the cake with the remaining frosting.

Drizzle with Salted Caramel Sauce:
- Drizzle additional salted caramel sauce over the top of the cake.
- Sprinkle a pinch of sea salt over the caramel drizzle for added flavor and decoration.

Serve:
- Slice the cake and serve. Enjoy the irresistible combination of sweet caramel and sea salt in every bite!

This salted caramel cake is a true indulgence and perfect for any special occasion or celebration. The rich caramel flavor paired with the moist cake layers and creamy frosting will surely impress your guests!

**Pumpkin Spice Cake**

Ingredients:

For the Cake:

- 2 cups all-purpose flour
- 1 teaspoon baking powder
- 1/2 teaspoon baking soda
- 1/2 teaspoon salt
- 2 teaspoons ground cinnamon
- 1/2 teaspoon ground ginger
- 1/4 teaspoon ground nutmeg
- 1/4 teaspoon ground cloves
- 1 cup pumpkin puree (not pumpkin pie filling)
- 1 cup granulated sugar
- 1/2 cup brown sugar, packed
- 1/2 cup vegetable oil
- 2 large eggs
- 1 teaspoon vanilla extract
- 1/2 cup buttermilk

For the Cream Cheese Frosting:

- 8 ounces cream cheese, softened
- 1/2 cup unsalted butter, softened
- 4 cups powdered sugar
- 1 teaspoon vanilla extract

Optional Garnish:

- Ground cinnamon or pumpkin pie spice for dusting

Instructions:

Preheat Oven and Prepare Pan:
- Preheat your oven to 350°F (175°C). Grease and flour a 9x13-inch baking pan or two 9-inch round cake pans.

Mix Dry Ingredients:

- In a medium bowl, whisk together the flour, baking powder, baking soda, salt, cinnamon, ginger, nutmeg, and cloves. Set aside.

Combine Wet Ingredients:
- In a large mixing bowl, whisk together the pumpkin puree, granulated sugar, brown sugar, vegetable oil, eggs, and vanilla extract until smooth.

Alternate Adding Dry Ingredients and Buttermilk:
- Gradually add the dry ingredients to the wet mixture, alternating with the buttermilk. Begin and end with the dry ingredients, mixing until just combined. Be careful not to overmix.

Bake:
- Pour the batter into the prepared baking pan(s) and spread it evenly. Bake in the preheated oven for 30-35 minutes (for a 9x13-inch pan) or 25-30 minutes (for round cake pans), or until a toothpick inserted into the center comes out clean.

Cool:
- Allow the cake to cool in the pan(s) for 10 minutes, then transfer it to a wire rack to cool completely.

Prepare Cream Cheese Frosting:
- In a large mixing bowl, beat together the softened cream cheese and unsalted butter until smooth and creamy.
- Gradually add the powdered sugar, 1 cup at a time, beating well after each addition.
- Beat in the vanilla extract until the frosting is smooth and fluffy.

Frost the Cake:
- Once the cake has cooled completely, spread the cream cheese frosting evenly over the top of the cake.

Optional Garnish:
- Sprinkle ground cinnamon or pumpkin pie spice over the frosting for a decorative touch.

Serve:
- Slice the cake and serve. Enjoy the warm and comforting flavors of pumpkin spice!

This pumpkin spice cake is perfect for autumn gatherings, holiday celebrations, or any time you're craving a taste of fall. The moist cake layers paired with creamy cream cheese frosting are sure to be a hit with family and friends!

**Gingerbread Cake**

Ingredients:

For the Cake:

- 2 1/4 cups all-purpose flour
- 1 teaspoon baking soda
- 1/2 teaspoon baking powder
- 1/2 teaspoon salt
- 1 tablespoon ground ginger
- 1 1/2 teaspoons ground cinnamon
- 1/4 teaspoon ground cloves
- 1/4 teaspoon ground nutmeg
- 1/2 cup unsalted butter, softened
- 1/2 cup granulated sugar
- 1/2 cup brown sugar, packed
- 2 large eggs
- 1 cup unsulfured molasses
- 1 cup hot water

For the Cream Cheese Frosting (Optional):

- 8 ounces cream cheese, softened
- 1/2 cup unsalted butter, softened
- 3-4 cups powdered sugar
- 1 teaspoon vanilla extract

Optional Garnish:

- Powdered sugar for dusting
- Candied ginger or whipped cream for serving

Instructions:

    Preheat Oven and Prepare Pan:
- Preheat your oven to 350°F (175°C). Grease and flour a 9x13-inch baking pan or two 9-inch round cake pans.

    Mix Dry Ingredients:

- In a medium bowl, whisk together the flour, baking soda, baking powder, salt, ginger, cinnamon, cloves, and nutmeg. Set aside.

Cream Butter and Sugars:
- In a large mixing bowl, cream together the softened butter, granulated sugar, and brown sugar until light and fluffy.

Add Eggs and Molasses:
- Beat in the eggs, one at a time, followed by the molasses, until well combined.

Combine Wet and Dry Ingredients:
- Gradually add the dry ingredients to the wet mixture, alternating with the hot water. Begin and end with the dry ingredients, mixing until just combined. Be careful not to overmix.

Bake:
- Pour the batter into the prepared baking pan(s) and spread it evenly. Bake in the preheated oven for 30-35 minutes (for a 9x13-inch pan) or 25-30 minutes (for round cake pans), or until a toothpick inserted into the center comes out clean.

Cool:
- Allow the cake to cool in the pan(s) for 10 minutes, then transfer it to a wire rack to cool completely.

Prepare Cream Cheese Frosting (Optional):
- In a large mixing bowl, beat together the softened cream cheese and unsalted butter until smooth and creamy.
- Gradually add the powdered sugar, 1 cup at a time, beating well after each addition.
- Beat in the vanilla extract until the frosting is smooth and fluffy.

Frost the Cake (Optional):
- Once the cake has cooled completely, spread the cream cheese frosting evenly over the top of the cake.

Garnish (Optional):
- Dust the top of the cake with powdered sugar before serving.
- Serve slices of cake with a garnish of candied ginger or a dollop of whipped cream, if desired.

Serve:
- Slice the cake and serve. Enjoy the comforting flavors of gingerbread!

This gingerbread cake is sure to evoke feelings of warmth and nostalgia, making it a perfect dessert for holiday gatherings or any cozy occasion.

**Almond Joy Cake**

Ingredients:

For the Cake:

- 2 cups all-purpose flour
- 1 cup granulated sugar
- 1 cup unsweetened cocoa powder
- 1 teaspoon baking powder
- 2 teaspoons baking soda
- 1 teaspoon salt
- 2 large eggs
- 1 cup buttermilk
- 1 cup strong brewed coffee, cooled
- 1/2 cup vegetable oil
- 2 teaspoons vanilla extract

For the Coconut Filling:

- 1 1/2 cups sweetened shredded coconut
- 1/2 cup sweetened condensed milk

For the Chocolate Ganache:

- 1 cup heavy cream
- 8 ounces semisweet chocolate chips
- 1 tablespoon unsalted butter

For the Topping:

- 1 cup whole almonds, toasted

Instructions:

    Preheat Oven and Prepare Pan:
- Preheat your oven to 350°F (175°C). Grease and flour three 9-inch round cake pans or line them with parchment paper.

    Mix Dry Ingredients:

- In a large mixing bowl, whisk together the flour, sugar, cocoa powder, baking powder, baking soda, and salt until well combined.

Combine Wet Ingredients:
- In another bowl, whisk together the eggs, buttermilk, cooled coffee, vegetable oil, and vanilla extract until smooth.

Combine Wet and Dry Ingredients:
- Gradually add the wet ingredients to the dry ingredients, mixing until just combined. Be careful not to overmix.

Divide Batter and Bake:
- Divide the batter evenly between the prepared cake pans. Smooth the tops with a spatula. Bake in the preheated oven for 25-30 minutes, or until a toothpick inserted into the center comes out clean.

Cool:
- Allow the cakes to cool in the pans for 10 minutes, then transfer them to a wire rack to cool completely.

Prepare Coconut Filling:
- In a small bowl, mix together the sweetened shredded coconut and sweetened condensed milk until well combined. Set aside.

Assemble the Cake:
- Place one cake layer on a serving plate or cake stand. Spread a layer of the coconut filling over the top.
- Place another cake layer on top and spread another layer of coconut filling. Repeat with the third cake layer.

Make Chocolate Ganache:
- In a small saucepan, heat the heavy cream until it just begins to simmer.
- Place the chocolate chips in a heatproof bowl. Pour the hot cream over the chocolate chips and let it sit for 2-3 minutes.
- Add the butter to the bowl and stir until the chocolate is melted and the ganache is smooth.

Frost the Cake with Chocolate Ganache:
- Pour the chocolate ganache over the top of the cake, allowing it to drip down the sides.
- Use an offset spatula to spread the ganache evenly over the top and sides of the cake.

Decorate with Almonds:
- Arrange the toasted almonds around the top edge of the cake as a border.

Chill and Serve:
- Refrigerate the cake for at least 30 minutes to set the ganache before serving. Slice and enjoy the delicious Almond Joy Cake!

This Almond Joy Cake is sure to be a hit at any gathering, with its rich chocolate layers, sweet coconut filling, and crunchy almond topping, reminiscent of the classic candy bar.

**Oreo Cookies and Cream Cake**

Ingredients:

For the Cake:

- 2 cups all-purpose flour
- 1 cup granulated sugar
- 1 cup unsweetened cocoa powder
- 1 teaspoon baking powder
- 2 teaspoons baking soda
- 1 teaspoon salt
- 2 large eggs
- 1 cup buttermilk
- 1 cup hot water
- 1/2 cup vegetable oil
- 2 teaspoons vanilla extract
- 1 cup crushed Oreo cookies (about 10-12 cookies)

For the Oreo Buttercream Frosting:

- 1 cup unsalted butter, softened
- 4 cups powdered sugar
- 1/4 cup milk
- 1 teaspoon vanilla extract
- 1 cup crushed Oreo cookies (about 10-12 cookies)

Optional Garnish:

- Whole Oreo cookies for decoration

Instructions:

Preheat Oven and Prepare Pan:
- Preheat your oven to 350°F (175°C). Grease and flour two 9-inch round cake pans or line them with parchment paper.

Mix Dry Ingredients:
- In a large mixing bowl, sift together the flour, sugar, cocoa powder, baking powder, baking soda, and salt. Mix well.

Combine Wet Ingredients:

- In another bowl, whisk together the eggs, buttermilk, hot water, vegetable oil, and vanilla extract until smooth.

Combine Wet and Dry Ingredients:
- Gradually add the wet ingredients to the dry ingredients, mixing until just combined. Be careful not to overmix.
- Fold in the crushed Oreo cookies until evenly distributed throughout the batter.

Divide Batter and Bake:
- Divide the batter evenly between the prepared cake pans. Smooth the tops with a spatula. Bake in the preheated oven for 25-30 minutes, or until a toothpick inserted into the center comes out clean.

Cool:
- Allow the cakes to cool in the pans for 10 minutes, then transfer them to a wire rack to cool completely.

Prepare Oreo Buttercream Frosting:
- In a large mixing bowl, beat the softened butter until creamy.
- Gradually add the powdered sugar, 1 cup at a time, alternating with the milk, until the frosting reaches your desired consistency.
- Beat in the vanilla extract until smooth.
- Fold in the crushed Oreo cookies until evenly distributed.

Assemble the Cake:
- Place one cake layer on a serving plate or cake stand. Spread a layer of Oreo buttercream frosting over the top.
- Place the second cake layer on top and frost the top and sides of the cake with the remaining frosting.

Decorate with Whole Oreo Cookies:
- Optionally, garnish the top of the cake with whole Oreo cookies for decoration.

Chill and Serve:
- Refrigerate the cake for at least 30 minutes to allow the frosting to set before serving.
- Slice and enjoy the delicious Oreo Cookies and Cream Cake!

This cake is perfect for Oreo lovers and special occasions. With its rich chocolate cake layers and creamy Oreo buttercream frosting, it's sure to be a crowd-pleaser!

**Chai Spice Cake**

Ingredients:

For the Cake:

- 2 cups all-purpose flour
- 1 1/2 teaspoons baking powder
- 1/2 teaspoon baking soda
- 1/2 teaspoon salt
- 2 teaspoons ground cinnamon
- 1 teaspoon ground ginger
- 1/2 teaspoon ground cardamom
- 1/2 teaspoon ground cloves
- 1/2 teaspoon ground nutmeg
- 1 cup granulated sugar
- 1/2 cup brown sugar, packed
- 3/4 cup unsalted butter, softened
- 3 large eggs
- 1 teaspoon vanilla extract
- 1 cup buttermilk

For the Chai Spice Buttercream Frosting:

- 1 cup unsalted butter, softened
- 4 cups powdered sugar
- 1-2 tablespoons milk or heavy cream
- 1 teaspoon ground cinnamon
- 1/2 teaspoon ground ginger
- 1/4 teaspoon ground cardamom
- 1/4 teaspoon ground cloves
- 1/4 teaspoon ground nutmeg
- 1 teaspoon vanilla extract

Optional Garnish:

- Cinnamon sticks or ground cinnamon for dusting

## Instructions:

### Preheat Oven and Prepare Pan:
- Preheat your oven to 350°F (175°C). Grease and flour two 9-inch round cake pans or line them with parchment paper.

### Mix Dry Ingredients:
- In a medium bowl, whisk together the flour, baking powder, baking soda, salt, cinnamon, ginger, cardamom, cloves, and nutmeg. Set aside.

### Cream Butter and Sugars:
- In a large mixing bowl, cream together the softened butter, granulated sugar, and brown sugar until light and fluffy.

### Add Eggs and Vanilla:
- Beat in the eggs, one at a time, followed by the vanilla extract, until well combined.

### Combine Wet and Dry Ingredients:
- Gradually add the dry ingredients to the wet mixture, alternating with the buttermilk. Begin and end with the dry ingredients, mixing until just combined. Be careful not to overmix.

### Divide Batter and Bake:
- Divide the batter evenly between the prepared cake pans. Smooth the tops with a spatula. Bake in the preheated oven for 25-30 minutes, or until a toothpick inserted into the center comes out clean.

### Cool:
- Allow the cakes to cool in the pans for 10 minutes, then transfer them to a wire rack to cool completely.

### Prepare Chai Spice Buttercream Frosting:
- In a large mixing bowl, beat the softened butter until creamy.
- Gradually add the powdered sugar, 1 cup at a time, alternating with the milk or heavy cream, until the frosting reaches your desired consistency.
- Beat in the ground cinnamon, ginger, cardamom, cloves, nutmeg, and vanilla extract until smooth and well combined.

### Assemble the Cake:
- Place one cake layer on a serving plate or cake stand. Spread a layer of chai spice buttercream frosting over the top.
- Place the second cake layer on top and frost the top and sides of the cake with the remaining frosting.

### Garnish (Optional):
- Garnish the top of the cake with cinnamon sticks or dust with ground cinnamon for an extra touch of chai spice flavor.

Serve:
- Slice the cake and serve. Enjoy the warm and aromatic flavors of chai spice cake!

This chai spice cake is perfect for any occasion, especially during the fall and winter months when you're craving cozy, comforting flavors. The combination of spices in the cake and frosting creates a deliciously unique dessert experience.

**Key Lime Cake**

Ingredients:

For the Cake:

- 2 cups all-purpose flour
- 1 teaspoon baking powder
- 1/2 teaspoon baking soda
- 1/2 teaspoon salt
- 1/2 cup unsalted butter, softened
- 1 cup granulated sugar
- 2 large eggs
- 1 teaspoon vanilla extract
- 1/2 cup key lime juice
- 1/2 cup buttermilk
- Zest of 2 key limes

For the Key Lime Glaze:

- 1/4 cup key lime juice
- 1/4 cup granulated sugar

For the Key Lime Cream Cheese Frosting:

- 8 ounces cream cheese, softened
- 1/2 cup unsalted butter, softened
- 4 cups powdered sugar
- 1/4 cup key lime juice
- Zest of 1-2 key limes

Optional Garnish:

- Slices of key lime
- Zest of key lime

Instructions:

Preheat Oven and Prepare Pan:

- Preheat your oven to 350°F (175°C). Grease and flour two 9-inch round cake pans or line them with parchment paper.

Mix Dry Ingredients:
- In a medium bowl, whisk together the flour, baking powder, baking soda, and salt. Set aside.

Cream Butter and Sugar:
- In a large mixing bowl, cream together the softened butter and granulated sugar until light and fluffy.

Add Eggs and Vanilla:
- Beat in the eggs, one at a time, followed by the vanilla extract, until well combined.

Alternate Adding Dry Ingredients and Wet Ingredients:
- Gradually add the dry ingredients to the wet mixture, alternating with the key lime juice and buttermilk. Begin and end with the dry ingredients, mixing until just combined. Be careful not to overmix.
- Fold in the key lime zest until evenly distributed throughout the batter.

Divide Batter and Bake:
- Divide the batter evenly between the prepared cake pans. Smooth the tops with a spatula. Bake in the preheated oven for 25-30 minutes, or until a toothpick inserted into the center comes out clean.

Cool:
- Allow the cakes to cool in the pans for 10 minutes, then transfer them to a wire rack to cool completely.

Prepare Key Lime Glaze:
- In a small saucepan, heat the key lime juice and granulated sugar over medium heat until the sugar has dissolved and the mixture has thickened slightly. Remove from heat and set aside.

Prepare Key Lime Cream Cheese Frosting:
- In a large mixing bowl, beat together the softened cream cheese and butter until smooth and creamy.
- Gradually add the powdered sugar, 1 cup at a time, until the frosting reaches your desired consistency.
- Beat in the key lime juice and zest until smooth and well combined.

Assemble the Cake:
- Place one cake layer on a serving plate or cake stand. Spread a layer of key lime cream cheese frosting over the top.
- Place the second cake layer on top and frost the top and sides of the cake with the remaining frosting.

Drizzle with Key Lime Glaze:

- Drizzle the key lime glaze over the top of the cake, allowing it to drip down the sides.

Garnish (Optional):
- Garnish the top of the cake with slices of key lime and additional zest for decoration.

Serve:
- Slice the cake and serve. Enjoy the tangy and refreshing flavors of key lime cake!

This key lime cake is perfect for any occasion, especially during the warmer months when you're craving something light and citrusy. The combination of tangy key lime flavor with creamy cream cheese frosting makes for a delightful dessert experience.

**Matcha Green Tea Cake**

Ingredients:

For the Cake:

- 2 cups all-purpose flour
- 2 tablespoons matcha green tea powder
- 1 1/2 teaspoons baking powder
- 1/2 teaspoon baking soda
- 1/2 teaspoon salt
- 1/2 cup unsalted butter, softened
- 1 1/4 cups granulated sugar
- 2 large eggs
- 1 teaspoon vanilla extract
- 1 cup buttermilk

For the Matcha Cream Cheese Frosting:

- 8 ounces cream cheese, softened
- 1/2 cup unsalted butter, softened
- 4 cups powdered sugar
- 2 tablespoons matcha green tea powder
- 1 teaspoon vanilla extract

Optional Garnish:

- Matcha powder for dusting
- Edible flowers or fresh berries

Instructions:

Preheat Oven and Prepare Pan:
- Preheat your oven to 350°F (175°C). Grease and flour two 9-inch round cake pans or line them with parchment paper.

Mix Dry Ingredients:
- In a medium bowl, whisk together the flour, matcha powder, baking powder, baking soda, and salt. Set aside.

Cream Butter and Sugar:

- In a large mixing bowl, cream together the softened butter and granulated sugar until light and fluffy.

Add Eggs and Vanilla:
- Beat in the eggs, one at a time, followed by the vanilla extract, until well combined.

Alternate Adding Dry Ingredients and Buttermilk:
- Gradually add the dry ingredients to the wet mixture, alternating with the buttermilk. Begin and end with the dry ingredients, mixing until just combined. Be careful not to overmix.

Divide Batter and Bake:
- Divide the batter evenly between the prepared cake pans. Smooth the tops with a spatula. Bake in the preheated oven for 25-30 minutes, or until a toothpick inserted into the center comes out clean.

Cool:
- Allow the cakes to cool in the pans for 10 minutes, then transfer them to a wire rack to cool completely.

Prepare Matcha Cream Cheese Frosting:
- In a large mixing bowl, beat together the softened cream cheese and butter until smooth and creamy.
- Gradually add the powdered sugar, 1 cup at a time, until the frosting reaches your desired consistency.
- Beat in the matcha powder and vanilla extract until smooth and well combined.

Assemble the Cake:
- Place one cake layer on a serving plate or cake stand. Spread a layer of matcha cream cheese frosting over the top.
- Place the second cake layer on top and frost the top and sides of the cake with the remaining frosting.

Garnish (Optional):
- Dust the top of the cake with matcha powder for a decorative touch.
- Garnish with edible flowers or fresh berries for an elegant presentation.

Serve:
- Slice the cake and serve. Enjoy the unique and delightful flavor of matcha green tea cake!

This matcha green tea cake is perfect for tea parties, celebrations, or any time you want to indulge in a sophisticated and flavorful dessert. The earthy matcha flavor combined with the creamy cream cheese frosting creates a harmonious and delicious cake experience.

**Mint Chocolate Chip Cake**

Ingredients:

For the Cake:

- 2 cups all-purpose flour
- 1 cup granulated sugar
- 1/2 cup unsweetened cocoa powder
- 1 teaspoon baking powder
- 1/2 teaspoon baking soda
- 1/2 teaspoon salt
- 2 large eggs
- 1 cup buttermilk
- 1/2 cup vegetable oil
- 1 teaspoon vanilla extract
- 1/2 teaspoon peppermint extract
- 1/2 cup mini chocolate chips

For the Mint Buttercream Frosting:

- 1 cup unsalted butter, softened
- 4 cups powdered sugar
- 1/4 cup milk or cream
- 1 teaspoon peppermint extract
- Green food coloring (optional)
- Additional mini chocolate chips for garnish

Instructions:

Preheat your oven to 350°F (175°C). Grease and flour two 9-inch round cake pans.
Prepare the Cake Batter:
- In a large mixing bowl, whisk together the flour, sugar, cocoa powder, baking powder, baking soda, and salt.
- Add eggs, buttermilk, vegetable oil, vanilla extract, and peppermint extract to the dry ingredients. Beat until well combined and smooth.
- Fold in the mini chocolate chips.

Bake the Cakes:
- Divide the batter evenly between the prepared cake pans.

- Bake in the preheated oven for 25-30 minutes or until a toothpick inserted into the center comes out clean.
- Remove from the oven and let the cakes cool in the pans for 10 minutes before transferring them to a wire rack to cool completely.

Prepare the Mint Buttercream Frosting:
- In a mixing bowl, beat the softened butter until creamy.
- Gradually add powdered sugar, one cup at a time, beating well after each addition.
- Add milk (or cream) and peppermint extract. Beat until smooth and creamy.
- If desired, add a few drops of green food coloring to achieve a minty green color.

Assemble the Cake:
- Once the cakes are completely cooled, place one layer on a serving plate or cake stand.
- Spread a layer of mint buttercream frosting over the top of the first cake layer.
- Place the second cake layer on top and frost the top and sides of the cake with the remaining frosting.
- Sprinkle additional mini chocolate chips on top of the cake for decoration.

Chill and Serve:
- For best results, chill the cake in the refrigerator for at least 30 minutes before serving to allow the frosting to set.
- Slice and serve your delicious mint chocolate chip cake, and enjoy!

This cake is perfect for any occasion, especially for mint and chocolate lovers!

**White Chocolate Raspberry Cake**

Ingredients:

For the cake:

- 2 cups all-purpose flour
- 1 teaspoon baking powder
- 1/2 teaspoon baking soda
- 1/4 teaspoon salt
- 1/2 cup unsalted butter, softened
- 1 cup granulated sugar
- 2 large eggs
- 1 teaspoon vanilla extract
- 1 cup buttermilk
- 6 ounces white chocolate, melted and cooled

For the raspberry filling:

- 2 cups fresh raspberries
- 1/4 cup granulated sugar
- 1 tablespoon cornstarch
- 1 tablespoon water

For the white chocolate ganache:

- 8 ounces white chocolate, chopped
- 1/2 cup heavy cream

Instructions:

Preheat your oven to 350°F (175°C). Grease and flour two 9-inch round cake pans.
Prepare the cake batter: In a medium bowl, whisk together flour, baking powder, baking soda, and salt. In a large mixing bowl, cream together butter and sugar until light and fluffy. Add eggs, one at a time, beating well after each addition. Stir in vanilla extract. Gradually add the dry ingredients to the creamed mixture, alternating with buttermilk. Stir in melted white chocolate until well combined.
Bake the cakes: Divide the batter evenly between the prepared cake pans. Smooth the tops with a spatula. Bake in the preheated oven for 25-30 minutes or until a toothpick inserted into the center comes out clean. Remove from the oven

and let the cakes cool in the pans for 10 minutes before transferring them to wire racks to cool completely.

Prepare the raspberry filling: In a small saucepan, combine raspberries, sugar, cornstarch, and water. Cook over medium heat, stirring constantly, until the mixture thickens and the raspberries break down, about 5-7 minutes. Remove from heat and let it cool completely.

Make the white chocolate ganache: Place chopped white chocolate in a heatproof bowl. In a small saucepan, heat the heavy cream until it just begins to simmer. Pour the hot cream over the white chocolate and let it sit for 2-3 minutes. Stir until the chocolate is completely melted and the mixture is smooth. Let it cool until it reaches a spreadable consistency.

Assemble the cake: Place one cake layer on a serving plate. Spread the raspberry filling evenly over the top. Place the second cake layer on top. Pour the white chocolate ganache over the cake, allowing it to drip down the sides. Use an offset spatula to spread the ganache evenly over the top and sides of the cake.

Chill the cake: Refrigerate the cake for at least 1 hour before serving to allow the ganache to set.

Serve: Slice and serve the cake, garnished with fresh raspberries if desired.

Enjoy your delicious white chocolate raspberry cake!

**Maple Pecan Cake**

Ingredients:

For the cake:

- 2 cups all-purpose flour
- 1 teaspoon baking powder
- 1/2 teaspoon baking soda
- 1/2 teaspoon salt
- 1/2 cup unsalted butter, softened
- 1 cup granulated sugar
- 2 large eggs
- 1 teaspoon vanilla extract
- 1 cup buttermilk
- 1/2 cup maple syrup
- 1 cup chopped pecans

For the maple pecan frosting:

- 1/2 cup unsalted butter, softened
- 1/2 cup maple syrup
- 2 cups powdered sugar
- 1 teaspoon vanilla extract
- 1/2 cup chopped pecans, toasted

Instructions:

Preheat your oven to 350°F (175°C). Grease and flour two 9-inch round cake pans.
Prepare the cake batter: In a medium bowl, whisk together flour, baking powder, baking soda, and salt. In a large mixing bowl, cream together butter and sugar until light and fluffy. Add eggs, one at a time, beating well after each addition. Stir in vanilla extract. Gradually add the dry ingredients to the creamed mixture, alternating with buttermilk and maple syrup. Stir in chopped pecans until evenly distributed.
Bake the cakes: Divide the batter evenly between the prepared cake pans. Smooth the tops with a spatula. Bake in the preheated oven for 25-30 minutes or until a toothpick inserted into the center comes out clean. Remove from the oven and let the cakes cool in the pans for 10 minutes before transferring them to wire racks to cool completely.
Prepare the maple pecan frosting: In a mixing bowl, beat together softened butter, maple syrup, powdered sugar, and vanilla extract until smooth and creamy.
Assemble the cake: Place one cake layer on a serving plate. Spread a layer of maple pecan frosting over the top. Place the second cake layer on top. Frost the top and sides of the cake with the remaining frosting.
Decorate with toasted pecans: Sprinkle the top of the cake with toasted chopped pecans for added flavor and decoration.

Chill the cake: Refrigerate the cake for at least 30 minutes before serving to allow the frosting to set.
Serve: Slice and serve the maple pecan cake, and enjoy the delightful combination of maple and pecan flavors!

This cake is perfect for any occasion, especially during the fall season when maple and pecan flavors are particularly popular.

**S'mores Cake**

Ingredients:

For the cake:

- 1 and 3/4 cups all-purpose flour
- 1 and 1/2 cups granulated sugar
- 3/4 cup unsweetened cocoa powder
- 1 and 1/2 teaspoons baking powder
- 1 and 1/2 teaspoons baking soda
- 1 teaspoon salt
- 2 large eggs, at room temperature
- 1 cup whole milk
- 1/2 cup vegetable oil
- 2 teaspoons vanilla extract
- 1 cup boiling water

For the marshmallow frosting:

- 4 large egg whites
- 1 cup granulated sugar
- 1/4 teaspoon cream of tartar
- 1 teaspoon vanilla extract

For assembling:

- 1 cup crushed graham crackers
- 1 cup mini marshmallows
- 1/2 cup semi-sweet chocolate chips or chunks

Instructions:

Preheat your oven to 350°F (175°C). Grease and flour two 9-inch round cake pans.

Prepare the cake batter: In a large mixing bowl, sift together flour, sugar, cocoa powder, baking powder, baking soda, and salt. Add eggs, milk, oil, and vanilla extract. Beat on medium speed until well combined. Reduce speed and carefully add boiling water to the cake batter. Beat on high speed for about 1 minute to add air to the batter.

Bake the cakes: Divide the batter evenly between the prepared cake pans. Bake for 30 to 35 minutes, or until a toothpick inserted into the center comes out clean. Remove from the oven and allow the cakes to cool completely in the pans.

Prepare the marshmallow frosting: In a heatproof bowl, combine egg whites, sugar, and cream of tartar. Place the bowl over a pot of simmering water, making sure the bottom of the bowl doesn't touch the water. Whisk constantly until the sugar is dissolved and the mixture is warm to the touch, about 3 to 4 minutes. Remove from heat.

Whip the frosting: Using a hand mixer or a stand mixer fitted with the whisk attachment, beat the mixture on high speed until stiff peaks form and the mixture has cooled to room temperature, about 5 to 7 minutes. Beat in vanilla extract until well combined.

Assemble the cake: Place one cake layer on a serving plate. Spread a layer of marshmallow frosting over the top. Sprinkle with crushed graham crackers, mini marshmallows, and chocolate chips. Place the second cake layer on top and repeat the process. Finish by spreading the remaining marshmallow frosting over the top and sides of the cake.

Optional: Use a kitchen torch to lightly toast the marshmallow frosting for that classic S'mores look and flavor.

Chill the cake: For best results, refrigerate the cake for about 30 minutes before serving to allow the frosting to set.

Serve: Slice and enjoy your delicious S'mores cake with friends and family!

This S'mores cake is sure to be a hit at any gathering, combining the flavors of a beloved campfire treat in a delightful cake form.

**Strawberry Champagne Cake**

Ingredients:

For the cake:

- 2 cups all-purpose flour
- 2 teaspoons baking powder
- 1/2 teaspoon salt
- 1/2 cup unsalted butter, softened
- 1 and 1/2 cups granulated sugar
- 3 large eggs, room temperature
- 1 teaspoon vanilla extract
- 1 cup champagne or sparkling wine
- 1/4 cup milk
- 1 cup finely chopped strawberries

For the champagne frosting:

- 1 and 1/2 cups unsalted butter, softened
- 5 cups powdered sugar
- 1/4 cup champagne or sparkling wine
- 1 teaspoon vanilla extract
- Fresh strawberries for garnish

Instructions:

Preheat your oven to 350°F (175°C). Grease and flour three 8-inch round cake pans.

Prepare the cake batter: In a medium bowl, whisk together flour, baking powder, and salt. In a separate large mixing bowl, cream together butter and sugar until light and fluffy. Add eggs one at a time, beating well after each addition. Stir in vanilla extract. Gradually add the dry ingredients to the creamed mixture, alternating with champagne and milk. Fold in chopped strawberries until evenly distributed.

Bake the cakes: Divide the batter evenly between the prepared cake pans. Smooth the tops with a spatula. Bake in the preheated oven for 25-30 minutes, or until a toothpick inserted into the center comes out clean. Remove from the oven and let the cakes cool in the pans for 10 minutes before transferring them to wire racks to cool completely.

Prepare the champagne frosting: In a large mixing bowl, beat softened butter until creamy. Gradually add powdered sugar, one cup at a time, beating well after each addition. Add champagne and vanilla extract, and beat until smooth and creamy.

Assemble the cake: Place one cake layer on a serving plate. Spread a layer of champagne frosting over the top. Repeat with the remaining cake layers and frosting, stacking them on top of each other. Use the remaining frosting to frost the top and sides of the cake.

Garnish: Decorate the top of the cake with fresh strawberries for an elegant finish.

Chill the cake: Refrigerate the cake for at least 30 minutes before serving to allow the frosting to set.

Serve: Slice and enjoy your delicious Strawberry Champagne Cake!

This cake is sure to impress with its delicate champagne flavor and bursts of fresh strawberry goodness. It's perfect for weddings, anniversaries, or any special occasion that calls for celebration.

**Earl Grey Tea Cake**

Ingredients:

For the cake:

- 2/3 cup milk
- 4 Earl Grey tea bags (or 2 tablespoons loose leaf Earl Grey tea)
- 1 and 3/4 cups all-purpose flour
- 1 and 1/2 teaspoons baking powder
- 1/4 teaspoon salt
- 1/2 cup unsalted butter, softened
- 1 cup granulated sugar
- 3 large eggs, room temperature
- 1 teaspoon vanilla extract
- Zest of 1 lemon (optional)

For the glaze:

- 1/4 cup freshly brewed strong Earl Grey tea (from about 2 tea bags)
- 1 and 1/2 cups powdered sugar

Instructions:

Preheat your oven to 350°F (175°C). Grease and flour a 9x5-inch loaf pan.
Infuse the milk with Earl Grey tea: In a small saucepan, heat the milk until it is steaming but not boiling. Remove from heat and add the Earl Grey tea bags (or loose leaf tea). Let the tea steep in the milk for about 10-15 minutes. Remove the tea bags or strain out the loose tea, pressing gently to extract as much flavor as possible. Allow the infused milk to cool to room temperature.
Prepare the cake batter: In a medium bowl, whisk together flour, baking powder, and salt. In a separate large mixing bowl, cream together butter and sugar until light and fluffy. Add eggs one at a time, beating well after each addition. Stir in vanilla extract and lemon zest (if using). Gradually add the dry ingredients to the creamed mixture, alternating with the infused milk, beginning and ending with the dry ingredients. Mix until just combined.
Bake the cake: Pour the batter into the prepared loaf pan and smooth the top with a spatula. Bake in the preheated oven for 45-55 minutes, or until a toothpick inserted into the center comes out clean. If the top of the cake starts to brown too quickly, you can tent it with aluminum foil halfway through baking.

Cool the cake: Allow the cake to cool in the pan for 10 minutes, then remove it from the pan and transfer it to a wire rack to cool completely.

Prepare the glaze: In a small bowl, whisk together the brewed Earl Grey tea and powdered sugar until smooth. If the glaze is too thick, you can add more tea, a teaspoon at a time, until you reach your desired consistency.

Glaze the cake: Once the cake has cooled completely, drizzle the glaze over the top of the cake. You can do this while the cake is still on the wire rack, with a piece of parchment paper underneath to catch any drips.

Serve: Slice and enjoy your delicious Earl Grey tea cake with a cup of tea or coffee!

This cake is perfect for tea time or as a sweet treat any time of day. The subtle floral notes of the Earl Grey tea complement the moist and tender crumb of the cake beautifully.

**Cinnamon Roll Cake**

Ingredients:

For the cake:

- 2 cups all-purpose flour
- 1 cup granulated sugar
- 2 teaspoons baking powder
- 1/2 teaspoon baking soda
- 1/2 teaspoon salt
- 1 cup buttermilk
- 2 large eggs
- 1/4 cup unsalted butter, melted
- 2 teaspoons vanilla extract

For the cinnamon swirl:

- 1/2 cup unsalted butter, softened
- 3/4 cup brown sugar, packed
- 2 tablespoons all-purpose flour
- 1 tablespoon ground cinnamon

For the cream cheese glaze:

- 4 ounces cream cheese, softened
- 1/4 cup unsalted butter, softened
- 1 cup powdered sugar
- 1 teaspoon vanilla extract
- 2-3 tablespoons milk, as needed to reach desired consistency

Instructions:

Preheat your oven to 350°F (175°C). Grease and flour a 9x13-inch baking dish.
Prepare the cinnamon swirl: In a small bowl, mix together softened butter, brown sugar, flour, and cinnamon until well combined. Set aside.
Prepare the cake batter: In a large mixing bowl, whisk together flour, sugar, baking powder, baking soda, and salt. In a separate bowl, whisk together buttermilk, eggs, melted butter, and vanilla extract until well combined. Pour the wet ingredients into the dry ingredients and mix until just combined, being careful not to overmix.

Assemble the cake: Pour half of the cake batter into the prepared baking dish and spread it out evenly. Dollop half of the cinnamon swirl mixture over the batter and swirl it into the batter using a knife or toothpick. Repeat with the remaining cake batter and cinnamon swirl mixture.

Bake the cake: Place the baking dish in the preheated oven and bake for 25-30 minutes, or until a toothpick inserted into the center of the cake comes out clean.

Make the cream cheese glaze: In a medium bowl, beat together softened cream cheese and butter until smooth and creamy. Add powdered sugar and vanilla extract, and beat until well combined. Gradually add milk, a tablespoon at a time, until the glaze reaches your desired consistency.

Glaze the cake: Once the cake has cooled slightly, drizzle the cream cheese glaze over the top of the cake.

Serve: Slice and enjoy your delicious Cinnamon Roll Cake warm or at room temperature. It's perfect for breakfast, brunch, or as a sweet treat any time of day!

This Cinnamon Roll Cake is sure to be a hit with its soft, fluffy texture and irresistible cinnamon swirls, topped with a creamy cream cheese glaze.

**Cranberry Orange Cake**

Ingredients:

For the cake:

- 2 cups all-purpose flour
- 1 teaspoon baking powder
- 1/2 teaspoon baking soda
- 1/2 teaspoon salt
- 1/2 cup unsalted butter, softened
- 1 cup granulated sugar
- 2 large eggs
- 1 teaspoon vanilla extract
- 1 cup plain yogurt or sour cream
- Zest of 1 orange
- 1 cup fresh cranberries, chopped

For the orange glaze:

- 1 cup powdered sugar
- 2-3 tablespoons fresh orange juice
- Zest of 1 orange (optional)

Instructions:

Preheat your oven to 350°F (175°C). Grease and flour a 9x5-inch loaf pan.
Prepare the cake batter: In a medium bowl, whisk together flour, baking powder, baking soda, and salt. In a separate large mixing bowl, cream together butter and sugar until light and fluffy. Add eggs one at a time, beating well after each addition. Stir in vanilla extract and orange zest. Gradually add the dry ingredients to the creamed mixture, alternating with yogurt or sour cream, beginning and ending with the dry ingredients. Mix until just combined. Fold in chopped cranberries.
Bake the cake: Pour the batter into the prepared loaf pan and smooth the top with a spatula. Bake in the preheated oven for 50-60 minutes, or until a toothpick inserted into the center comes out clean. If the top of the cake starts to brown too quickly, you can tent it with aluminum foil halfway through baking.
Cool the cake: Allow the cake to cool in the pan for 10 minutes, then remove it from the pan and transfer it to a wire rack to cool completely.

Prepare the orange glaze: In a small bowl, whisk together powdered sugar and fresh orange juice until smooth. If the glaze is too thick, you can add more orange juice, a teaspoon at a time, until you reach your desired consistency. Stir in orange zest if desired.

Glaze the cake: Once the cake has cooled completely, drizzle the orange glaze over the top of the cake. You can do this while the cake is still on the wire rack, with a piece of parchment paper underneath to catch any drips.

Serve: Slice and enjoy your delicious Cranberry Orange Cake with a cup of tea or coffee!

This cake is perfect for any occasion, with its vibrant flavors and moist, tender crumb. The combination of cranberries and orange is both refreshing and festive, making it a wonderful choice for holidays or special gatherings.

**Neapolitan Cake**

Ingredients:

For the chocolate cake layer:

- 1 and 1/2 cups all-purpose flour
- 1 cup granulated sugar
- 1/3 cup unsweetened cocoa powder
- 1 teaspoon baking soda
- 1/2 teaspoon salt
- 1 cup water
- 1/3 cup vegetable oil
- 1 tablespoon white vinegar
- 1 teaspoon vanilla extract

For the vanilla cake layer:

- 1 and 1/2 cups all-purpose flour
- 1 cup granulated sugar
- 1 teaspoon baking powder
- 1/2 teaspoon baking soda
- 1/2 teaspoon salt
- 1/2 cup unsalted butter, softened
- 2 large eggs
- 3/4 cup buttermilk
- 1 teaspoon vanilla extract

For the strawberry cake layer:

- 1 and 1/2 cups all-purpose flour
- 1 cup granulated sugar
- 1 teaspoon baking powder
- 1/2 teaspoon baking soda
- 1/4 teaspoon salt
- 1/2 cup unsalted butter, softened
- 2 large eggs
- 1/2 cup buttermilk
- 1/2 cup strawberry puree (made from fresh or frozen strawberries)

For the frosting:

- 1 and 1/2 cups unsalted butter, softened
- 6 cups powdered sugar
- 1/4 cup heavy cream
- 1 teaspoon vanilla extract
- 1/2 cup strawberry puree
- Pink food coloring (optional)

Instructions:

Preheat your oven to 350°F (175°C). Grease and flour three 9-inch round cake pans.

Prepare the chocolate cake layer: In a large mixing bowl, whisk together flour, sugar, cocoa powder, baking soda, and salt. Add water, vegetable oil, vinegar, and vanilla extract. Mix until smooth. Divide the batter evenly between two of the prepared cake pans. Bake for 25-30 minutes, or until a toothpick inserted into the center comes out clean. Remove from the oven and let cool in the pans for 10 minutes before transferring to wire racks to cool completely.

Prepare the vanilla cake layer: In a large mixing bowl, cream together softened butter and sugar until light and fluffy. Add eggs one at a time, beating well after each addition. Stir in buttermilk and vanilla extract. In a separate bowl, whisk together flour, baking powder, baking soda, and salt. Gradually add the dry ingredients to the wet ingredients, mixing until just combined. Divide the batter evenly between one of the prepared cake pans. Bake for 25-30 minutes, or until a toothpick inserted into the center comes out clean. Remove from the oven and let cool in the pan for 10 minutes before transferring to a wire rack to cool completely.

Prepare the strawberry cake layer: In a large mixing bowl, cream together softened butter and sugar until light and fluffy. Add eggs one at a time, beating well after each addition. Stir in buttermilk and strawberry puree. In a separate bowl, whisk together flour, baking powder, baking soda, and salt. Gradually add the dry ingredients to the wet ingredients, mixing until just combined. Divide the batter evenly between the remaining prepared cake pan. Bake for 25-30 minutes, or until a toothpick inserted into the center comes out clean. Remove from the oven and let cool in the pan for 10 minutes before transferring to a wire rack to cool completely.

Prepare the frosting: In a large mixing bowl, beat softened butter until creamy. Gradually add powdered sugar, one cup at a time, beating well after each addition. Add heavy cream and vanilla extract, and beat until smooth and creamy. Divide the frosting into three portions. Leave one portion plain, and mix the second portion with strawberry puree until well combined. Add pink food coloring to the third portion to achieve the desired shade of pink.

Assemble the cake: Place the chocolate cake layer on a serving plate. Spread a layer of chocolate frosting over the top. Place the vanilla cake layer on top and spread a layer of vanilla frosting over the top. Place the strawberry cake layer on top and spread a layer of strawberry frosting over the top. Repeat the process with the remaining frosting, spreading chocolate frosting over the sides of the cake, vanilla frosting around the middle, and strawberry frosting on top.

Decorate: Use a spatula to create a smooth finish on the frosting. You can also pipe decorative designs on top if desired.

Chill the cake: For best results, refrigerate the cake for at least 30 minutes before serving to allow the frosting to set.

Serve: Slice and enjoy your delicious Neapolitan Cake with layers of chocolate, vanilla, and strawberry goodness!

This cake is perfect for celebrations or any special occasion, with its beautiful layers and delightful combination of flavors.

**Pineapple Coconut Cake**

Ingredients:

For the cake:

- 2 cups all-purpose flour
- 1 and 1/2 teaspoons baking powder
- 1/2 teaspoon baking soda
- 1/2 teaspoon salt
- 1/2 cup unsalted butter, softened
- 1 cup granulated sugar
- 3 large eggs
- 1 teaspoon vanilla extract
- 1 cup canned crushed pineapple, drained
- 1/2 cup shredded coconut
- 1/2 cup buttermilk

For the coconut frosting:

- 1 and 1/2 cups unsweetened shredded coconut
- 1 and 1/2 cups sweetened shredded coconut
- 1/2 cup unsalted butter, softened
- 8 ounces cream cheese, softened
- 4 cups powdered sugar
- 1 teaspoon vanilla extract
- 2-3 tablespoons milk (as needed to reach desired consistency)

Instructions:

Preheat your oven to 350°F (175°C). Grease and flour two 9-inch round cake pans.
Prepare the cake batter: In a medium bowl, whisk together flour, baking powder, baking soda, and salt. In a separate large mixing bowl, cream together butter and sugar until light and fluffy. Add eggs one at a time, beating well after each addition. Stir in vanilla extract. Fold in crushed pineapple and shredded coconut. Gradually add the dry ingredients to the creamed mixture, alternating with buttermilk, beginning and ending with the dry ingredients. Mix until just combined.
Bake the cakes: Divide the batter evenly between the prepared cake pans. Smooth the tops with a spatula. Bake in the preheated oven for 25-30 minutes, or

until a toothpick inserted into the center comes out clean. Remove from the oven and let the cakes cool in the pans for 10 minutes before transferring them to wire racks to cool completely.

Prepare the coconut frosting: Spread the shredded coconut on a baking sheet and toast in the preheated oven for about 5-7 minutes, stirring occasionally, until golden brown. Set aside to cool.

In a large mixing bowl, beat together softened butter and cream cheese until smooth and creamy. Gradually add powdered sugar, one cup at a time, beating well after each addition. Add vanilla extract and mix until smooth. If the frosting is too thick, add milk, one tablespoon at a time, until you reach your desired consistency. Stir in 1 cup of toasted shredded coconut.

Assemble the cake: Place one cake layer on a serving plate. Spread a layer of coconut frosting over the top. Place the second cake layer on top and frost the top and sides of the cake with the remaining frosting. Sprinkle the remaining toasted shredded coconut over the top of the cake.

Chill the cake: For best results, refrigerate the cake for at least 1 hour before serving to allow the frosting to set.

Serve: Slice and enjoy your delicious Pineapple Coconut Cake, and savor the tropical flavors!

This cake is perfect for summer gatherings, birthdays, or any occasion where you want to bring a taste of the tropics to the table. Enjoy!

**Chocolate Peanut Butter Swirl Cake**

Ingredients:

For the chocolate cake:

- 1 and 3/4 cups all-purpose flour
- 3/4 cup unsweetened cocoa powder
- 2 cups granulated sugar
- 1 and 1/2 teaspoons baking powder
- 1 and 1/2 teaspoons baking soda
- 1 teaspoon salt
- 2 large eggs
- 1 cup buttermilk
- 1/2 cup vegetable oil
- 2 teaspoons vanilla extract
- 1 cup hot water

For the peanut butter swirl:

- 1 cup creamy peanut butter
- 1/4 cup powdered sugar
- 2 tablespoons unsalted butter, softened

For the chocolate glaze (optional):

- 1 cup semi-sweet chocolate chips
- 1/2 cup heavy cream
- 2 tablespoons unsalted butter

Instructions:

Preheat your oven to 350°F (175°C). Grease and flour a 9x13-inch baking dish. Prepare the chocolate cake batter: In a large mixing bowl, whisk together flour, cocoa powder, sugar, baking powder, baking soda, and salt. Add eggs, buttermilk, vegetable oil, and vanilla extract. Beat on medium speed until well combined. Gradually add hot water and mix until the batter is smooth.
Prepare the peanut butter swirl: In a small bowl, mix together creamy peanut butter, powdered sugar, and softened butter until smooth and well combined.
Assemble the cake: Pour half of the chocolate cake batter into the prepared baking dish and spread it out evenly. Dollop spoonfuls of the peanut butter swirl mixture over the chocolate batter. Use a knife or skewer to gently swirl the peanut

butter mixture into the chocolate batter. Pour the remaining chocolate cake batter over the top and smooth it out with a spatula.

Bake the cake: Place the baking dish in the preheated oven and bake for 35-40 minutes, or until a toothpick inserted into the center comes out clean. Remove from the oven and let the cake cool completely in the pan.

Prepare the chocolate glaze (optional): In a small saucepan, heat heavy cream until it just begins to simmer. Remove from heat and add chocolate chips and unsalted butter. Let it sit for 2-3 minutes, then stir until the chocolate is completely melted and the mixture is smooth.

Glaze the cake (optional): Once the cake has cooled, pour the chocolate glaze over the top of the cake and spread it out evenly with a spatula.

Chill the cake: For best results, refrigerate the cake for at least 30 minutes before serving to allow the glaze to set.

Serve: Slice and enjoy your delicious Chocolate Peanut Butter Swirl Cake!

This cake is perfect for chocolate and peanut butter lovers alike, with its rich chocolate flavor and swirls of creamy peanut butter. It's sure to be a hit at any gathering or special occasion!

**Caramel Apple Cake**

Ingredients:

For the cake:

- 2 cups all-purpose flour
- 1 and 1/2 teaspoons baking powder
- 1/2 teaspoon baking soda
- 1/2 teaspoon salt
- 1 teaspoon ground cinnamon
- 1/4 teaspoon ground nutmeg
- 1/2 cup unsalted butter, softened
- 1 cup granulated sugar
- 2 large eggs
- 1 teaspoon vanilla extract
- 1/2 cup sour cream or Greek yogurt
- 2 cups finely chopped apples (about 2 medium apples)

For the caramel sauce:

- 1 cup granulated sugar
- 6 tablespoons unsalted butter, cut into pieces
- 1/2 cup heavy cream
- 1 teaspoon vanilla extract
- Pinch of salt

Instructions:

Preheat your oven to 350°F (175°C). Grease and flour a 9x9-inch square baking pan or a 9-inch round cake pan.

Prepare the cake batter: In a medium bowl, whisk together flour, baking powder, baking soda, salt, cinnamon, and nutmeg. In a separate large mixing bowl, cream together softened butter and sugar until light and fluffy. Add eggs one at a time, beating well after each addition. Stir in vanilla extract. Gradually add the dry ingredients to the creamed mixture, alternating with sour cream or Greek yogurt, beginning and ending with the dry ingredients. Mix until just combined. Fold in chopped apples.

Bake the cake: Pour the batter into the prepared baking pan and smooth the top with a spatula. Bake in the preheated oven for 35-40 minutes, or until a toothpick inserted into the center comes out clean. Remove from the oven and let the cake cool in the pan for 10 minutes before transferring it to a wire rack to cool completely.

Prepare the caramel sauce: In a medium saucepan, heat granulated sugar over medium heat, stirring constantly with a high heat resistant rubber spatula or wooden spoon. Sugar will form clumps and eventually melt into a thick brown, amber-colored liquid as you continue to stir. Be careful not to burn.

Once sugar is completely melted, immediately add the butter. Be careful in this step because the caramel will bubble rapidly when the butter is added. Stir the butter into the caramel until it is completely melted, about 2-3 minutes.

Very slowly, drizzle in the heavy cream while stirring. Since the heavy cream is colder than the caramel, the mixture will rapidly bubble and/or splatter when added. Allow the mixture to boil for 1 minute. It will rise in the pan as it boils. Remove from heat and stir in vanilla extract and salt. Allow caramel sauce to cool down before using.

Assemble the cake: Once the cake has cooled, drizzle the caramel sauce over the top of the cake. You can also pour some caramel sauce between the layers if desired.

Serve: Slice and enjoy your delicious Caramel Apple Cake, and savor the wonderful combination of sweet caramel and tart apples!

This cake is perfect for fall gatherings, holidays, or any occasion where you want to indulge in a sweet and comforting dessert.

**Eggnog Cake**

Ingredients:

For the cake:

- 2 and 1/4 cups all-purpose flour
- 2 teaspoons baking powder
- 1/2 teaspoon baking soda
- 1/2 teaspoon salt
- 1 teaspoon ground nutmeg
- 1/2 cup unsalted butter, softened
- 1 cup granulated sugar
- 3 large eggs
- 1 teaspoon vanilla extract
- 1 cup eggnog
- 1/4 cup rum or bourbon (optional)

For the eggnog glaze:

- 1 cup powdered sugar
- 2-3 tablespoons eggnog
- 1/2 teaspoon vanilla extract
- Pinch of ground nutmeg

For garnish (optional):

- Additional ground nutmeg
- Whipped cream
- Cinnamon sticks

Instructions:

Preheat your oven to 350°F (175°C). Grease and flour a 9x13-inch baking dish or two 8-inch round cake pans.

Prepare the cake batter: In a medium bowl, whisk together flour, baking powder, baking soda, salt, and nutmeg. In a separate large mixing bowl, cream together softened butter and sugar until light and fluffy. Add eggs one at a time, beating well after each addition. Stir in vanilla extract. Gradually add the dry ingredients to the creamed mixture, alternating with eggnog and rum or bourbon (if using), beginning and ending with the dry ingredients. Mix until just combined.

Bake the cake: Pour the batter into the prepared baking dish or cake pans and smooth the top with a spatula. Bake in the preheated oven for 25-30 minutes (for the 9x13-inch dish) or 30-35 minutes (for the round cake pans), or until a toothpick inserted into the center comes out clean. Remove from the oven and let the cake cool in the pan(s) for 10 minutes before transferring it to a wire rack to cool completely.

Prepare the eggnog glaze: In a small bowl, whisk together powdered sugar, eggnog, vanilla extract, and a pinch of nutmeg until smooth and creamy. If the glaze is too thick, you can add more eggnog, a tablespoon at a time, until you reach your desired consistency.

Glaze the cake: Once the cake has cooled completely, drizzle the eggnog glaze over the top of the cake. You can do this while the cake is still in the pan(s) or after transferring it to a serving platter.

Garnish (optional): Sprinkle additional ground nutmeg over the top of the glazed cake. Serve slices of eggnog cake with whipped cream and cinnamon sticks for a festive touch.

Serve: Slice and enjoy your delicious Eggnog Cake, and savor the creamy, spiced flavors of the holiday season!

This cake is perfect for holiday gatherings, Christmas parties, or any occasion where you want to indulge in the comforting flavors of eggnog.

**Peppermint Chocolate Cake**

Ingredients:

For the chocolate cake:

- 1 and 3/4 cups all-purpose flour
- 3/4 cup unsweetened cocoa powder
- 2 cups granulated sugar
- 1 and 1/2 teaspoons baking powder
- 1 and 1/2 teaspoons baking soda
- 1 teaspoon salt
- 2 large eggs
- 1 cup buttermilk
- 1/2 cup vegetable oil
- 2 teaspoons vanilla extract
- 1 cup hot water

For the peppermint frosting:

- 1 cup unsalted butter, softened
- 4 cups powdered sugar
- 1/4 cup milk
- 1 teaspoon peppermint extract
- Crushed candy canes or peppermint candies, for garnish

Instructions:

Preheat your oven to 350°F (175°C). Grease and flour two 9-inch round cake pans.

Prepare the chocolate cake batter: In a large mixing bowl, whisk together flour, cocoa powder, sugar, baking powder, baking soda, and salt. Add eggs, buttermilk, vegetable oil, and vanilla extract. Beat on medium speed until well combined. Gradually add hot water and mix until the batter is smooth.

Bake the cakes: Divide the batter evenly between the prepared cake pans. Smooth the tops with a spatula. Bake in the preheated oven for 30-35 minutes, or until a toothpick inserted into the center comes out clean. Remove from the oven and let the cakes cool in the pans for 10 minutes before transferring them to wire racks to cool completely.

Prepare the peppermint frosting: In a large mixing bowl, beat softened butter until creamy. Gradually add powdered sugar, one cup at a time, beating well after each addition. Add milk and peppermint extract, and beat until smooth and creamy. If the frosting is too thick, you can add more milk, a tablespoon at a time, until you reach your desired consistency.

Assemble the cake: Once the cakes have cooled completely, place one cake layer on a serving plate. Spread a layer of peppermint frosting over the top. Place the second cake layer on top and frost the top and sides of the cake with the remaining frosting.

Garnish: Sprinkle crushed candy canes or peppermint candies over the top of the frosted cake for a festive touch.

Serve: Slice and enjoy your delicious Peppermint Chocolate Cake, and savor the wonderful combination of rich chocolate and refreshing peppermint flavors!

This cake is perfect for holiday parties, Christmas gatherings, or any occasion where you want to indulge in a festive and flavorful dessert.

**Bourbon Pecan Cake**

Ingredients:

For the cake:

- 1 and 1/2 cups chopped pecans
- 2 cups all-purpose flour
- 1 teaspoon baking powder
- 1/2 teaspoon baking soda
- 1/2 teaspoon salt
- 1/2 cup unsalted butter, softened
- 1 and 1/2 cups granulated sugar
- 3 large eggs
- 1/2 cup sour cream
- 1/4 cup bourbon
- 1 teaspoon vanilla extract

For the bourbon glaze:

- 1/4 cup unsalted butter
- 1/2 cup granulated sugar
- 1/4 cup bourbon

Instructions:

Preheat your oven to 350°F (175°C). Grease and flour a 9x13-inch baking dish or a Bundt pan.

Toast the pecans: Spread the chopped pecans on a baking sheet and toast them in the preheated oven for 8-10 minutes, or until fragrant. Remove from the oven and let them cool.

Prepare the cake batter: In a medium bowl, whisk together flour, baking powder, baking soda, and salt. In a separate large mixing bowl, cream together softened butter and sugar until light and fluffy. Add eggs one at a time, beating well after each addition. Stir in sour cream, bourbon, and vanilla extract. Gradually add the dry ingredients to the creamed mixture, mixing until just combined. Fold in the toasted pecans.

Bake the cake: Pour the batter into the prepared baking dish or Bundt pan and spread it out evenly. Bake in the preheated oven for 35-40 minutes (for the 9x13-inch dish) or 45-50 minutes (for the Bundt pan), or until a toothpick inserted

into the center comes out clean. Remove from the oven and let the cake cool in the pan for 10 minutes before transferring it to a wire rack to cool completely.
Prepare the bourbon glaze: In a small saucepan, melt butter over medium heat. Stir in sugar and bourbon. Bring to a boil, then reduce heat and simmer for 5 minutes, stirring constantly, until the glaze thickens slightly.
Glaze the cake: Once the cake has cooled completely, drizzle the bourbon glaze over the top of the cake. You can do this while the cake is still in the pan or after transferring it to a serving platter.
Serve: Slice and enjoy your delicious Bourbon Pecan Cake, and savor the rich flavors of bourbon and pecans!

This cake is perfect for special occasions, holiday gatherings, or any time you want to indulge in a decadent and flavorful dessert.

**Cookies and Cream Cupcakes**

Ingredients:

- 1 and 1/2 cups all-purpose flour
- 1 teaspoon baking powder
- 1/2 teaspoon baking soda
- 1/4 teaspoon salt
- 1/2 cup unsalted butter, softened
- 1 cup granulated sugar
- 2 large eggs
- 1 teaspoon vanilla extract
- 1/2 cup sour cream
- 1/2 cup whole milk
- 12 Oreo cookies, crushed (plus more for garnish)

For the frosting:

- 1/2 cup unsalted butter, softened
- 2 cups powdered sugar
- 2-3 tablespoons whole milk
- 1 teaspoon vanilla extract
- 6 Oreo cookies, crushed (for topping)

Instructions:

Preheat your oven to 350°F (175°C). Line a 12-cup muffin tin with cupcake liners. Prepare the cupcake batter: In a medium bowl, whisk together flour, baking powder, baking soda, and salt. In a large mixing bowl, cream together softened butter and sugar until light and fluffy. Add eggs one at a time, beating well after each addition. Stir in vanilla extract. Gradually add the dry ingredients to the creamed mixture, alternating with sour cream and milk, beginning and ending with the dry ingredients. Mix until just combined. Fold in crushed Oreo cookies. Fill the cupcake liners: Divide the batter evenly among the prepared muffin cups, filling each about 2/3 full.
Bake the cupcakes: Place the muffin tin in the preheated oven and bake for 18-20 minutes, or until a toothpick inserted into the center comes out clean. Remove from the oven and let the cupcakes cool in the tin for 5 minutes before transferring them to a wire rack to cool completely.
Prepare the frosting: In a large mixing bowl, beat softened butter until creamy. Gradually add powdered sugar, one cup at a time, beating well after each

addition. Add milk and vanilla extract, and beat until smooth and creamy. Fold in crushed Oreo cookies.

Frost the cupcakes: Once the cupcakes have cooled completely, frost them with the cookies and cream frosting. You can do this with a piping bag fitted with a decorating tip or simply use a spatula to spread the frosting on top of each cupcake.

Garnish: Sprinkle additional crushed Oreo cookies over the frosted cupcakes for garnish.

Serve: Enjoy your delicious Cookies and Cream Cupcakes!

**Strawberry Cheesecake Cupcakes**

Ingredients:

- 1 and 1/2 cups graham cracker crumbs
- 1/4 cup granulated sugar
- 1/2 cup unsalted butter, melted
- 16 ounces cream cheese, softened
- 1/2 cup granulated sugar
- 2 large eggs
- 1 teaspoon vanilla extract
- 1/2 cup sour cream
- 1/2 cup strawberry preserves or jam

Instructions:

Preheat your oven to 350°F (175°C). Line a 12-cup muffin tin with cupcake liners.
Prepare the crust: In a small bowl, mix together graham cracker crumbs, sugar, and melted butter until well combined. Press about 1 tablespoon of the mixture into the bottom of each cupcake liner.
Prepare the cheesecake filling: In a large mixing bowl, beat softened cream cheese until smooth. Add sugar and beat until creamy. Add eggs one at a time, beating well after each addition. Stir in vanilla extract and sour cream until well combined.
Fill the cupcake liners: Spoon about 2 tablespoons of the cheesecake filling over the graham cracker crust in each cupcake liner.
Add strawberry preserves: Drop about 1 teaspoon of strawberry preserves or jam onto the top of each cheesecake-filled cupcake liner. Use a toothpick to gently swirl the preserves into the cheesecake filling.
Bake the cupcakes: Place the muffin tin in the preheated oven and bake for 18-20 minutes, or until the cheesecake is set and the edges are lightly golden. Remove from the oven and let the cupcakes cool in the tin for 5 minutes before transferring them to a wire rack to cool completely.
Chill and serve: Once the cupcakes have cooled completely, refrigerate them for at least 1 hour before serving to allow the cheesecake to set. Enjoy your delicious Strawberry Cheesecake Cupcakes!

These cupcakes are perfect for parties, gatherings, or any time you want to enjoy a delightful dessert with friends and family.

**Lemon Blueberry Cupcakes**

Ingredients:

For the cupcakes:

- 1 and 1/2 cups all-purpose flour
- 1 and 1/2 teaspoons baking powder
- 1/4 teaspoon salt
- 1/2 cup unsalted butter, softened
- 1 cup granulated sugar
- 2 large eggs
- 1 teaspoon vanilla extract
- Zest of 1 lemon
- 1/4 cup fresh lemon juice
- 1/2 cup buttermilk
- 1 cup fresh blueberries (tossed in 1 tablespoon flour to prevent sinking)

For the lemon cream cheese frosting:

- 1/2 cup unsalted butter, softened
- 8 ounces cream cheese, softened
- 4 cups powdered sugar
- Zest of 1 lemon
- 2 tablespoons fresh lemon juice
- 1 teaspoon vanilla extract

For garnish:

- Fresh blueberries
- Lemon zest

Instructions:

Preheat your oven to 350°F (175°C). Line a 12-cup muffin tin with cupcake liners. Prepare the cupcakes: In a medium bowl, whisk together flour, baking powder, and salt. In a separate large mixing bowl, cream together softened butter and sugar until light and fluffy. Add eggs one at a time, beating well after each addition. Stir in vanilla extract and lemon zest. Gradually add the dry ingredients to the creamed mixture, alternating with buttermilk and lemon juice, beginning and ending with the dry ingredients. Mix until just combined. Gently fold in the blueberries.

Fill the cupcake liners: Divide the batter evenly among the prepared muffin cups, filling each about 2/3 full.

Bake the cupcakes: Place the muffin tin in the preheated oven and bake for 18-20 minutes, or until a toothpick inserted into the center comes out clean. Remove from the oven and let the cupcakes cool in the tin for 5 minutes before transferring them to a wire rack to cool completely.

Prepare the lemon cream cheese frosting: In a large mixing bowl, beat softened butter and cream cheese until smooth and creamy. Gradually add powdered sugar, one cup at a time, beating well after each addition. Stir in lemon zest, lemon juice, and vanilla extract until well combined.

Frost the cupcakes: Once the cupcakes have cooled completely, frost them with the lemon cream cheese frosting. You can do this with a piping bag fitted with a decorating tip or simply use a spatula to spread the frosting on top of each cupcake.

Garnish: Top each cupcake with a few fresh blueberries and a sprinkle of lemon zest for garnish.

Serve: Enjoy your delicious Lemon Blueberry Cupcakes!

These cupcakes are perfect for any occasion, from brunches to parties, with their bright and refreshing flavor combination.

**Salted Caramel Cupcakes**

Ingredients:

For the cupcakes:

- 1 and 1/2 cups all-purpose flour
- 1 and 1/2 teaspoons baking powder
- 1/4 teaspoon salt
- 1/2 cup unsalted butter, softened
- 1 cup granulated sugar
- 2 large eggs
- 1 teaspoon vanilla extract
- 1/2 cup whole milk

For the salted caramel sauce:

- 1 cup granulated sugar
- 6 tablespoons unsalted butter, cut into pieces
- 1/2 cup heavy cream
- 1 teaspoon vanilla extract
- 1/2 teaspoon sea salt (plus extra for garnish)

For the frosting:

- 1/2 cup unsalted butter, softened
- 2 cups powdered sugar
- 1/4 cup salted caramel sauce (cooled)

Instructions:

Preheat your oven to 350°F (175°C). Line a 12-cup muffin tin with cupcake liners. Prepare the cupcakes: In a medium bowl, whisk together flour, baking powder, and salt. In a separate large mixing bowl, cream together softened butter and sugar until light and fluffy. Add eggs one at a time, beating well after each addition. Stir in vanilla extract. Gradually add the dry ingredients to the creamed mixture, alternating with milk, beginning and ending with the dry ingredients. Mix until just combined.

Fill the cupcake liners: Divide the batter evenly among the prepared muffin cups, filling each about 2/3 full.

Bake the cupcakes: Place the muffin tin in the preheated oven and bake for 18-20 minutes, or until a toothpick inserted into the center comes out clean. Remove from the oven and let the cupcakes cool in the tin for 5 minutes before transferring them to a wire rack to cool completely.

Prepare the salted caramel sauce: In a medium saucepan, heat granulated sugar over medium heat, stirring constantly with a high heat resistant rubber spatula or wooden spoon. Sugar will form clumps and eventually melt into a thick brown, amber-colored liquid as you continue to stir. Be careful not to burn.

Once sugar is completely melted, immediately add the butter. Be careful in this step because the caramel will bubble rapidly when the butter is added. Stir the butter into the caramel until it is completely melted, about 2-3 minutes.

Very slowly, drizzle in the heavy cream while stirring. Since the heavy cream is colder than the caramel, the mixture will rapidly bubble and/or splatter when added. Allow the mixture to boil for 1 minute. It will rise in the pan as it boils. Remove from heat and stir in vanilla extract and sea salt. Allow caramel sauce to cool down before using.

Prepare the frosting: In a large mixing bowl, beat softened butter until creamy. Gradually add powdered sugar, one cup at a time, beating well after each addition. Add salted caramel sauce (cooled) and beat until smooth and creamy.

Frost the cupcakes: Once the cupcakes have cooled completely, frost them with the salted caramel frosting. You can do this with a piping bag fitted with a decorating tip or simply use a spatula to spread the frosting on top of each cupcake.

Garnish: Sprinkle a pinch of sea salt over the top of each frosted cupcake for garnish.

Serve: Enjoy your delicious Salted Caramel Cupcakes!

These cupcakes are perfect for special occasions, parties, or any time you want to indulge in a decadent and flavorful dessert.

www.ingramcontent.com/pod-product-compliance
Lightning Source LLC
LaVergne TN
LVHW081556060526
838201LV00054B/1914